Ghost Lights

And Other Encounters with the Unknown

Ghost Lights

And Other Encounters with the Unknown

E. Randall Floyd

August House Publishers, Inc.
LITTLE ROCK

Printed in the United States of America

10 9 8 7 6 5 4 3 2 1

LIBRARY OF CONGRESS CATALOGING-IN-PUBLICATION DATA

Floyd, E. Randall
Ghost lights and other encounters with the unknown / E. Randall Floyd
— 1st ed.
p.   cm.
Includes bibliographical references.
ISBN 0-87483-310-8 : $19.95
ISBN 0-87483-311-6 : $9.95
1. Curiosities and wonders—United States—Anecdotes. I. Title.

E179.F659 1993
001.9′4—dc20   93-20327

First Edition, 1993

Executive: Liz Parkhurst
Project editor: Kathleen Harper
Design director: Ted Parkhurst
Cover design: Byron Taylor
Typography: Lettergraphics/Little Rock

This book is printed on archival-quality paper which meets the
guidelines for performance and durability of the Committee on
Production Guidelines for Book Longevity of the
Council on Library Resources.

AUGUST HOUSE, INC.   PUBLISHERS   LITTLE ROCK

*This book is for Rand,
who taught me a lot about patience.*

Contents

Ghostly Incursions

Miracles and Visions

Fantastic Beasts

Unearthly Encounters

Bizarre Theories

History's Mysteries

Untimely Endings

Unusual Characters

Selected Bibliography

The oldest and strongest emotion of mankind is fear, and the oldest and strongest kind of fear is fear of the unknown.
—*Howard Phillips Lovecraft*

We—or our primitive forefathers—once believed that the return of the dead, unseen forces, and secret injurious powers were realities, and were convinced that they actually happened. Nowadays we no longer believe in them, we have surmounted those modes of thought; but we do not feel quite sure of our new beliefs, and the old ones still exist within us ready to seize upon any confirmation.
—*Sigmund Freud*

A first encounter with any grand fantastic theory, not political or economic, delights me.
—*J.B. Priestley*

Ghostly Incursions

Cry of the Banshee

JAMES O'BARRY HAD GOOD REASON to believe something was wrong when he was awakened early one morning by a loud, shrieking noise that reminded him of an "old, demented woman crying."

He was, after all, a good Irish Catholic, the son of a Boston grocer. And, like most members of his clan, young O'Barry believed in the legends of the fairy woman—or banshee, as the spirit is commonly called in Ireland, the land of his ancestry—a creature capable of foretelling death.

It was in the spring and O'Barry, then only ten years old, had been lying in bed listening to the birds singing outside his window.

That's when he heard it—a pathetic wailing sound that shattered the still morning air.

"It sent chills down my spine," O'Barry later recalled.

He pulled back the curtains and peeked out the window.

"The sun was shining and the sky was blue," O'Barry explained. "I thought for a moment or two that the wind had sprung up, but a glance at the barely stirring trees told me that this was not so."

O'Barry got up, went downstairs, and found his father sitting at the kitchen table with tears in his eyes. That seemed most unusual, because O'Barry had never before seen his father cry.

Then his mother came into the room, a grim expression on her face.

"Son," his mother said softly, "we've just heard by telephone that your grandfather has died in New York."

O'Barry, who went on to become the successful owner of a chain of supermarkets throughout New England, never forgot the strange incident. It was, he later wrote, "as if some spirit from the other side had been trying to warn me in advance of my grandfather's death."

Years later, while stationed with the U.S. Air Force in the Far East, O'Barry heard the eerie sound a second time. Only this time, instead of a high-pitched shrieking wail, it was a low howling that he heard, somewhere just outside his window.

"That time," he recalled, "I was instantly aware of what it was."

He sat bolt upright in bed, hair bristling on the back of his neck as he listened to the frightful noise.

"The noise got louder, rising and falling like an air raid siren," he wrote. "Then it died away, and I realized that I was terribly depressed. I knew my father was dead."

A few days later, O'Barry was notified that his father had died in an automobile accident.

The strangest portent was yet to come.

Seventeen years after the howling sound had interrupted his morning rest to warn him of his father's impending death, O'Barry would hear the disturbing melody a third time. He was on a business trip in Canada, alone, lying in bed reading the morning paper.

As he recalled, "Again ... a dreadful noise was suddenly filling my ears. I thought of my wife, my young son, my two brothers, and I thought, 'Good God, don't let it be one of them.'"

It wasn't.

The date was November 22, 1963.

The banshee that came to O'Barry that morning was bewailing the death of an acquaintance of O'Barry—John F. Kennedy, president of the United States.

Banshees—or *bansidhe*, 'fairy women' in Gaelic—have long been a part of the Irish folk tradition. According to legend, the banshee, regarded as a female guardian spirit in Wales, Scotland, and other parts of the British Isles, attaches itself to a family and watches over them throughout their life.

The creature, though rarely seen as an apparition, is usually described as a red-haired, green-eyed woman whose mournful cry foretells death. In Wales she is known as the "dribbling hag." In Scotland, the "death woman" can sometimes be seen lurking on the banks of rivers, washing the clothes of those about to die.

British history is full of stories about banshees roaming the open moors, lighting up the night sky with their fiery eyes and wings. Ancient kings and queens listened to the spirit's mournful wail before going off into battle.

During medieval times, nearly every prominent family in the Gaelic world had its own guardian angel—or banshee—to watch over its fortunes and foibles.

James O'Barry's horrifying ordeal was apparently the first time that a banshee had crossed the Atlantic to America.

Alice of the Hermitage

OF ALL THE GREAT GHOST STORIES of the Deep South, none is more beguiling than that of Alice Flagg, the beautiful young Carolina belle whose tormented spirit is said to still haunt the lonely marshes and live oak glades surrounding her ancestral homestead near Myrtle Beach.

Since Alice's death more than 140 years ago, scores of people claim to have seen her ghost—usually described as a frail young woman dressed in a shimmering white dress—floating serenely across the lawn or cemetery where her body is allegedly buried, or occasionally hovering in front of a mirror in her bedroom.

One visitor to Alice's home—a sprawling plantation-style showplace known locally as the Hermitage—swore she awoke one night to find the ghastly form of the long-dead girl standing at the foot of her bed.

Another said he heard her footsteps going up and down the stairway all night long, while yet another insisted she heard her singing or weeping outside the window late one night.

Among the visitors who claimed to have experienced psychic revelations at the Hermitage were movie actress Patricia Neal and her husband, writer Roald Dahl.

The story of Alice Flagg began in 1850 when the sixteen-year-old daughter of well-to-do rice planters Ebenezer and Margaret Elizabeth Belin Flagg came down with hemor-rhagic fever, a mosquito-related disease linked to the deaths of hundreds of islanders each year. About the same time, her aristocratic family was horrified to discover the girl was secretly engaged to a common turpentine worker from Charleston.

When Dr. Allard Flagg—Alice's brother and attending physician—found the engagement ring around her neck, legend has it he either threw it away or sent it back to the young man.

It was at that point, according to researcher Genevieve Peterkin, that Alice became delirious with fever and kept begging for her ring back.

"In an attempt to quiet her, Allard took his own ring and put it on her hand," Mrs. Peterkin said. "Just before the girl died, however, she pulled her brother's ring from her finger and said, 'Keep your ring, Allard. I shall find mine in death.'"

Alice was buried in the front yard of her plantation home for a short time before being moved to the graveyard of a nearby Episcopalian church. The family marked her grave with a marble stone, but Alice's engagement had disgraced them so much that her slab was denied the dignity of the family name. The only word on the stone is "Alice."

Today, visitors to the moss-shrouded cemetery often comment on the eerie silence and drifting shadows. Some say that if you walk around the grave thirteen times, Alice's ghost will appear.

Until his death a few years back, Clarke Wilcox, an old-timer whose family bought the Hermitage in 1910, used to entertain visitors by telling them stories about Alice's ghost. Part of his performance was to lead guests upstairs to Alice's bedroom, which has remained virtually unchanged, even after all these years.

The same furniture is there, and so is the view from the gabled window of the marshy grasses and shallow waters of the inlet facing the house. On a wall near the window is the portrait of a young girl—Alice Flagg on her sixteenth birthday. It has been described as "one of the most beautiful faces that was ever put on canvas."

Even with bright sunlight streaming through the window, the immediate impression one receives upon entering that room is that he is not alone.

"Sometimes I can't feel her presence at all," Wilcox once told a reporter. "But at other times I know she's there."

Wilcox said a lot of visitors—"especially young ones"—don't like to sign the guest register at the Hermitage for fear Alice's ghost will track them down.

Another visitor arriving by automobile once told Wilcox that he had passed a lovely young girl on the way up the circular, magnolia-scented driveway. The girl was dressed in white, the visitor told Wilcox, but when he stopped to talk to her she disappeared.

"Oh, it was just Alice," the old man cackled, "out taking a stroll."

The Ghost That Built a Railroad

YOUNG ARTHUR STILWELL'S PARENTS were stunned when he walked into the house one day and declared that he had quit his low-paying job and planned to move out west with his new bride.

They were even more surprised when he told them why: ghostly voices inside his head had commanded him to do so.

"In the West," the voices had said, "you will find your destiny. You will truly become one of this nation's great captains of industry."

Stilwell moved west, just as he had been commanded by the voices, built a railroad, and became one of America's richest and most powerful tycoons. He also found success as a writer, churning out more than thirty books, all of them bestsellers.

In what has to be one of the eeriest testimonials on record, the millionaire author would later credit his success to the strange voices inside his head.

But the mysterious voices that had commanded him to move west were nothing new to young Stilwell. In fact, the voices had been with him for as long as he could remember, guiding him and instructing him along life's way.

As a four-year-old child, he had once remarked to his mother, "I like the people in my head, but they make me so angry sometimes because they won't come out and let me see them."

While still a youngster in school, the same voices had told him he would grow up and marry a girl named Jennie Wood.

Even more compelling was their prediction that he would marry the girl within four years!

At the time he had never even heard of Jennie Wood. But four short years later, after having met the girl at a party, the couple indeed became husband and wife.

The eerie voices stayed with Stilwell for the rest of his life. In time they formed such an integral part of his personality that he couldn't have kept them a secret even had he wanted to. And, as he accumulated millions building railroads and cranking out one best-selling book after another, he often enjoyed delighting his friends and family members with stories about his "unseen companions."

His road to fame and fortune had opened up that morning at his parents' home when he announced that he and Jennie were moving to the Wild West town of Kansas City. It was there, he told them, that the voices had told him to go; it was there, he said, that he would make his fortune.

Once in Kansas City, the voices came to him again, advising him what to do next.

Young Stilwell, who had already begun to write stories and dream of making money in business, relayed the information to his wife.

"I am to build railroads," he said.

"Railroads?" Jennie gasped. "But how? With what? We have no money."

The millionaire-to-be couldn't answer his wife's questions. The truth was, he hadn't the foggiest notion how to put together any kind of business, let alone a complex operation like a railroad. Railroads, he knew, required enormous sums of planning and capital. With no money in his pocket and no wealthy family members to draw from, how on earth was he going to do it? Could the voices have made a mistake this time?

The answer came to him in a flash—backers! He would ask wealthy men to pump start-up capital into the project.

It all seemed so simple, but would it really work?

The next day he started calling on potential investors. Within weeks he had managed to put together a small group of investment partners whose infusion of capital enabled him to launch the Kansas City Belt Line railroad. The line would later expand into a sprawling network of rails that covered fifteen thousand square miles of track.

As the railway grew, so did Stilwell's remarkable success as a writer. Year after year, as new lines opened up under his control, he cranked out a steady stream of bestsellers. Arthur Stilwell, rich, famous, handsome, and happy, soon became the toast of the western literary and business world.

In 1900 he was busy putting together new plans to construct a railroad linking Kansas with the Gulf of Mexico when the voices came to him again. They told him to stop construction at once, that danger and "a cloud of disaster" lay ahead.

Without hesitation, Stilwell rerouted the terminal line from Galveston, Texas, to a mosquito-infested wasteland that would later be named Port Arthur in his own honor. On September 8, 1900, a mighty hurricane slammed into Galveston, nearly obliterating the city.

Stilwell had listened to the voices and narrowly averted the "cloud of disaster."

Never once did he doubt the wisdom of the voices again. In 1910, based on information provided by his "unseen companions," he predicted World War I. He also prophesied the defeat of Germany, the rise of Hitler, the collapse of the Russian czar, and the rise of Communism.

In 1928 the voices spoke to him one last time. Lying on his deathbed, he took his wife's hand and urged her to be strong. "The voices have been telling me again to protect you," he whispered. "You must be brave and try not to join me too soon."

This time Jennie ignored both her husband and the strange voices inside his head. Two weeks after his funeral, she jumped to her own death from a New York skyscraper, summoned, some say, by her late husband's mysterious voices.

The Case of the Haunted Newspaper

WHEN MOST PEOPLE THINK OF GHOSTS and hauntings, their thoughts usually turn to steep-gabled houses, drafty old castles, and mist-shrouded graveyards.

Rarely do newspaper offices come to mind. It's hard to associate the clean clatter of linotype machines and the electronic hum of modern video terminals with rattling chains, moaning noises, and phantom footsteps echoing down unlit hallways.

But don't try to tell that to the people who work for the Sulliven County *News*. Some reporters, editors, and other staffers of the Blountsville, Tennessee, weekly claim the place is haunted.

For the past four decades, *News* workers have told harrowing stories about doors opening and closing mysteriously, linotype machines suddenly starting up by themselves, eerie whistling sounds echoing through the basement, and spectral shadows flitting across the newsroom.

One former editor was so unnerved he grabbed his pistol and fired twice at something he thought was a ghost.

"And we're all the time missing things," complained June Eaton, the advertising supervisor. "They'll be there, and all of a sudden, you won't see them—scissors, flowers, pencils, anything."

Thelma Harrington, another former editor, said she was working in the darkroom alone one night when she heard a strange, whistling sound. Thinking it was a friend, she went outside to investigate.

"I opened the door and called his name," she said. "He didn't respond. I looked out in the parking lot and his car wasn't there. So I went back into the darkroom, and the whistling started again."

After searching the entire building, she simply concluded that "nobody ... was there."

Other witnesses include Glen and Melvin Boyd, brothers who worked as printers until their retirement several years ago. Both tell of constantly hearing footsteps clomping around at night on the upper floor, while they were working down below in the print shop.

Each time they went up to investigate they found the door locked and no one there. Their encounters with the unknown were shared by many others who told of similar experiences.

In fact, the mysterious sounds on the first floor became so common, especially late at night, that most workers stopped going up to investigate.

"I must have gone up a hundred times," Melvin said. "and there was nobody there. Usually we didn't bother to go upstairs. In fact, if somebody actually had come in, the people downstairs would be very startled."

One of the most bizarre encounters involved a young editor who had just started work at the paper. According to Glen Boyd, the editor was working late one night when he heard the linotype machine start up by itself.

"He (the editor) thought it was me," said Boyd, "and he came down to talk to me. But I was out covering a story. When he got downstairs nobody was there. But now he could hear something upstairs, someone walking around. He went upstairs, but there was no one there and he went back to his office."

At that moment the front door suddenly sprang open by itself, Boyd explained.

"It got to a point where it shook him up," Boyd went on. "He had a pistol in his desk drawer, and he got it out and went out into the main room. He didn't see anybody, but the newspaper files were moving, as though somebody were flipping through them. He had a little .25 automatic gun and he had his finger on the trigger, and it went off twice, putting two bullet holes in the ceiling. The marks are still there."

Some people say they have actually seen the ghost known around the office as "George." A former printer named Jim Gose once described a tall, slender man dressed in a gray suit who came into the office through the back door, walked ten steps toward the stairs, went upstairs, and then vanished.

Other witnesses claim to have seen apparitions. Thelma Harrington, the former editor, is one of them.

"One time," she said, "I saw a person in the office across the hall from my office. It appeared to be a young man with blond hair and a crew cut, which was not usual for that time—crew cuts were long past. He was wearing a white oxford shirt and blue pants with pleats in front. All of that stuff was completely out of style at that time."

A quick check through the rest of the building turned up nothing, she added—the whole place was empty!

Predictably, theories abound as to the origin and nature of the ghost. The most popular notion is that the apparition is that of a young man said to have been killed back in the 1940s when the newspaper building was a pool hall.

The best time to witness the ghost, say those *News* staffers who believe, is late at night and on weekends, when few people are around. One investigator, Arthur Myers, author of *The Ghostly Gazetteer*, reports that manifestations can be experienced any time of day or night.

"The opening and closing front door seems to happen often during usual working hours," according to Myers. "The footsteps are more discernible during the evening or on weekends, when only one or two people are in the building."

The Devil Made Her Do It

GINA HAD ALWAYS BEEN a healthy, happy teenager who enjoyed dating, going to movies, and reading books. Like most of her friends, the sixteen-year-old looked forward to finishing high school and going off to college.

But in the autumn of 1990, all of that changed when something ghastly entered the girl's life—something so bizarre it would take an ancient ritual of the Roman Catholic Church to make the girl approach anything near normalcy.

At first nobody noticed the subtle changes creeping over the girl. Except for a few uncustomary mood swings, Gina continued to behave like any other normal teenager.

Then one day her mother caught the girl on her hands and knees howling like an animal.

"I was terrified," the distraught mother later explained. "She was spitting and vomiting and screaming about demons inside her head."

Not only that, "her eyes were bulging, her face was red and blotchy and she was tearing at her hair like a wild animal."

Eventually the girl calmed down, but in the next few days there were other alarming signs that something was seriously wrong with the teenager, including her sudden fascination with the diabolic and her aversion to anything of a religious nature.

According to Gina's mother, "she began to hear voices all the time, animal voices, and she began to grow more and more violent and to speak in strange tongues."

More extraordinary were the physical contortions the girl underwent.

"Gina became strong—so strong I was afraid of her," the mother noted. "We had to restrain her with ropes sometimes."

The final straw came when the girl levitated across the room—in full view of several family members.

"She just rose from her chair and floated across the room," Gina's mother said.

After the levitation episode, family members took the girl to a psychic healer who interpreted the symptoms at once: the girl was obviously possessed by the devil.

The only way to free her from the demonic grip, he advised, was through the ancient ritual of exorcism.

"You can imagine how I felt about that," the mother said. "I didn't want to believe it. It couldn't be true, not my daughter."

But when her daughter's behavior worsened, the woman called in a priest. After several examinations by the priest and other specialists, including some skeptical psychiatrists, an exorcism was recommended.

The ritual of exorcism is as ancient as it is controversial. The Greeks and Romans, as well as peoples of the Bible, often called upon holy men to use their powers to cleanse victims possessed by demons.

"The devil does exist," noted Father James LeBar, who participated in Gina's exorcism. "He is a fallen angel, capable of possessing minds and making them do evil."

The Roman Catholic Church recognizes four signs of possession: strength, levitation, clairvoyance, and the ability to speak in strange languages.

Gina's unusual strength, her ability to "float" across the room, to anticipate future events, and to speak in foreign tongues convinced observers she was indeed possessed.

When ABC News learned of the story, it got permission from the Roman Catholic Church to film the rare and ancient ritual. The six-hour exorcism ordeal was condensed to half an hour and broadcast to millions of startled viewers courtesy of ABC's "20-20" news show.

According to ABC, it was one of the highest-rated shows in television history. While millions watched, Gina writhed and screamed and shrieked, guided by a team of priests, psychiatrists, doctors, and nurses.

Television commentators compared the attempt to cleanse the teenager of demonic possession with scenes from *The Exorcist*, the 1973 film that thrilled and terrorized millions of moviegoers.

During the ritual, it was determined that no fewer than ten spirits had invaded the girl's body, two of which were identified as "Minga" and "Zion," both African in origin. Pressing a crucifix against Gina's forehead, the priest—identified as "Father A"—commanded the spirits to leave the girl.

"In the name of Jesus Christ, the cross compels you to leave," the priest intoned repeatedly.

Speaking through Gina, the spirits replied: "We don't want to leave.... Stay away from me!"

"Do you want to be free of these demons?" Father A asked Gina.

"Yes," the girl replied in a cracking voice.

"Then kiss the cross of Christ!"

Several hours later the brood of demons apparently departed from their shackled young host.

"It's over," the priest told Gina. "You can go home now."

But was it truly over?

"We're not really sure," Gina's mother explained. "She's on the road to recovery, but she still hears the voices sometimes."

To be on the safe side, a priest was sent to Gina's house to exorcise the place of evil spirits. As for Gina, she continues to be treated with antipsychotic tranquilizers and therapy.

"But I feel much better," she explained. "God has liberated me from evil, and those voices … don't bother me anymore."

This House Possessed

IN THE HEART OF ONE of Washington, D.C.'s, most fashionable neighborhoods stands an old stone dwelling that many claim is the most dangerously haunted house in America.

For as long as anyone can remember, the house—built in pre-Revolutionary War times by a Pennsylvania cabinet maker—has been center stage for some of the most bizarre supernatural antics on record.

According to witnesses, unfriendly spirits stalking the gloomy corridors of the steeply gabled structure located at 3051 M Street NW have repeatedly tried to seriously injure or even kill visitors. One victim claims a ghost actually tried to push her off of a second-floor balcony.

While some may scoff at such remarks, one woman is convinced of their veracity. Her name is Rae Koch. Rae is the park ranger in charge of the house, which was purchased by the National Park Service in 1950 and converted into a museum.

"So far, in the twenty-four years I've been here I've seen eight ghosts in the house," Rae said. "They're all different kinds, all different time periods."

The star performer is a terrifying presence known to the staff as George. George, who inhabits a third-floor bedroom and frequently can be seen wandering along the upstairs hallway, hates women and occasionally gets violent.

He has been accused of attempting to strangle women, knife them, rape them, and even to push some of them over a railing outside his room or down the stairs.

"There's a ghost in that bedroom who's a real stinker," Rae explained. "He's one of those self-righteous, you-do-as-I-say types. It's not a nice feeling up there."

It is Rae, in fact, who claims to have nearly been pushed over a railing by the unseen spirit.

"I was standing by the railing there one night (with a friend), and I got an effect of being pushed over the rail, that someone was trying to push me over," she noted.

Her friend, a respected investigator of paranormal phenomena who spends a lot of time at the Old Stone House, supported the park ranger's testimony.

"We could sense the presence of the entity," the parapsychologist said, asking that his real name not be used. "It had form. I could feel the thing. Rae was complaining of a pressure on her right side, and I grabbed her and pulled her away from the railing."

Another encounter with George nearly cost volunteer guide Karen Cobb her life.

"He almost killed me," she noted. "I worked there a number of years and I had a lot of strange things happen to me, but this was unusual because it was so violent."

According to Karen, the near-tragic incident occurred late one night while she was showing an English friend around upstairs. They had just sat down on a bed when suddenly "I ... felt this impression on the bed next to me."

She turned to her friend and asked: "Do you feel that?"

When her friend nodded apprehensively, Karen reached over and became aware of an "ice-cold" presence.

"The next thing I knew there were hands around my throat, strangling me, like from behind, and I couldn't get loose," Karen explained. "I ended up just struggling and breaking free. I ran downstairs. I ran outside the house and it was like it was pursuing me till I got outside in the yard."

There, on a pile of bricks, Karen collapsed. "My throat was bruised badly. Finally, I got my breath back, and I thought, I'm not going back up there!"

Several visitors—none of whom were aware of the ghostly inhabitants of the Old Stone House—have complained of icy sensations entering their bodies, leading some investigators to conclude they were being "knifed" by some sinister force without actually drawing blood.

Witnesses have described dozens of other spirits wandering about the house besides George. They include that of a Civil War-era woman who sits in a rocker on the third floor, a little boy who runs up and down the third-floor hallway, two gentlemen from the colonial period, a young girl with ringlets in her hair, a German-looking craftsman, and that of a small black boy.

The ghosts appear to come and go at will, without regard for time of day or night. They stroll down corridors, stand idly by the kitchen fireplace, play on the steep stairwell, and occasionally materialize in bedrooms.

Except for George, none of the other spirits appears to be dangerous.

Rae and some other investigators theorize that one of the ghosts is that of Georgetown Mayor Robert Peter, who owned the house at the time of the American Revolution. Another ghost haunting the three-story, L-shaped structure might be that of Peter's mistress, for whom the mayor bought the house.

Like most haunted houses, the Old Stone House has a long and colorful history—in this case, stretching back to the mid-eighteenth century. Thought to be the site of Sutter's Tavern—where George Washington and Pierre L'Enfant once laid out plans for the city of Washington—the building has also been used as a private residence, auto body shop, and popular bordello.

The handsome old structure has been completely restored and contains much of its original period furnishings. According to one psychic investigator, the pristine condition of the house probably explains why so many spirits still cling to the place.

"The reconstruction here did very little to alter the interior," he said. "Many key pieces are there from the original house. There is a very pure environment there. It is as though the life of the house stopped dead in 1950."

Old Hickory and the Bell Witch

ANDREW JACKSON, THE SEVENTH PRESIDENT of the United States, was not a superstitious man.

But in 1820, eight years before he moved into the White House, the rugged old Indian fighter and hero of New Orleans came face to face with a power that would challenge his views of the unknown.

It happened near his plantation home in Tennessee. In those days, much of the state was wild and remote, and old stories and legends about "spirits of the earth" abounded. These spirits were said to be mostly benign and some actually helpful to the hard-working pioneers of the lonely forests and mountains.

But occasionally tales cropped up about less friendly spirits, malign spirits that sought to harm and destroy rather than help and instruct.

Such was the nature of the uninvited spirit that came to the home of the Bell family in 1818.

For months, ever since he'd purchased the old farm from Jackson, John Bell and his family had been bothered by an eerie voice that seemed to come from within the walls of the house. At first they thought it was the wind, then later, rats.

One day, in the presence of several astonished onlookers, the voice spoke. "I am a spirit who was once happy," the voice said in a cackling, female tone. "But now I have been disturbed and am unhappy."

The spirit identified herself as a witch of the forest who had once lived on the land "long, long ago." She informed her listeners that she was haunting the Bell farm because someone had disturbed her bones.

"My bones were buried near here," the spirit said. "And I want them back."

Although Bell succeeded in finding what he believed were the old woman's bones and providing them with a proper Christian burial, the annoying spirit refused to leave the family alone. If anything, it seemed to make matters worse.

In the days that followed, the witch proceeded to torment Bell—first causing his tongue to swell until he could barely eat, drink, or speak. His physical condition quickly deteriorated as the old witch continued to torment him.

One attending physician said, "We have seen nothing like it in our experience of morbid and pathological conditions. There appears to be no known reason for the affliction and there is certainly no known cure."

Bell didn't recover. Instead, he grew steadily worse as unseen hands slapped him sharply across the face, ripped clothes from his body, and punched him in the stomach. Sometimes the witch kicked him in the legs, and on one occasion she even spat in his face.

"I've almost done with you, Jack Bell," the witch proclaimed. "It won't be long now before you go to your grave to rot!"

Investigators, neighbors, and members of Bell's family begged the old spirit to release the farmer from her wrath. One of the neighbors who sought to rescue Bell from the clutches of the evil hag was Andrew Jackson himself.

Determined to do what he could—perhaps even expose the notorious witch as a hoax—"Old Hickory," as he was sometimes called, decided to spend the night in the Bell house. But after only a few hours inside that haunted dwelling, Jackson became convinced the horrors were real.

His first confrontation with the witch came at dinner. He had just settled down at the table with a glass of wine when a disembodied voice shrieked from the shadows, "How's that fat old wife of yours? Think you'll ever get Rachel's swollen carcass into the White House?"

Rachel was Jackson's wife. Their marriage had been clouded for some time because of a technicality in Rachel's divorce from her first husband. Some called her an adulteress because she and Jackson had married before the divorce decree had been finalized.

The controversy over their marriage would lead to bitter quarrels and even a deadly duel between Jackson and at least one political enemy. The last thing he would tolerate was ridicule of his beloved Rachel.

But how could he duel with a ghost?

For the rest of the night, the poltergeist romped through the house, taunting the despondent future president with her ugly jokes about "fat old Rachel."

A few days later, John Bell died—murdered, said his family, by the wicked witch. At his funeral the voice of the Bell witch was heard one last time, cackling and croaking triumphantly over the farmer's death.

And then, just as mysteriously as she had appeared, she was gone forever.

As for Jackson, he would never forget his grim encounter with the infamous Bell witch of Tennessee.

The Troubled President from beyond the Grave

ON THE NIGHT OF MAY 27, 1955, former president Harry S. Truman went on national television to reveal a shocking secret.

While an estimated fifty million Americans looked on, Truman told interviewer Edward R. Murrow that a ghost stalked the drafty corridors of the White House.

It was no ordinary ghost, either.

"I think it's the ghost of Abraham Lincoln walking around," the president said calmly into the camera, "perhaps here to warn me about something."

Ever since his arrival at the White House ten years earlier, Truman said, he had been bothered by a strange tapping noise on the other side of the presidential bedroom doors. The sound, described as "unusually sad and melancholy," usually came to him late at night or early in the morning.

Most often it would happen around 3:00 A.M. while the rest of the White House slept. As the president told it, he'd be awakened by the knocking sound beyond the doors. He'd crawl out of bed, fling open the doors, and peer down both sides of the hallway.

The result would always be the same: nothing.

"There was no one there," he explained, "so I'd go back to bed."

In bed, he'd think about all the old legends which told how Lincoln—who was fifty-five when he died—prowled the drafty corridors of the White House, moving from room to orderly room, a tormented look in his eyes and a plaid shawl draped around his craggy shoulders.

According to old reports, Lincoln had seen his own death in a dream at least twice. He also had visions about other unworldly events, a gift supposedly handed down to him by his psychic mother. Night after night, disturbing and significant symbols and premonitions came to him in his sleep, and he found that he was greatly troubled by his conscience.

Among the things Lincoln claimed to have seen was "the knowledge of and ... the power to change the future." As a youth growing up in a backwoods log cabin near Hodgen's Mill in what is now Larue County, Kentucky, Lincoln felt it wiser to keep his psychic powers to himself.

But just about everybody who knew him was aware of the ill-fated president's amazing ability to "see" into the future and predict events without knowing how he was able to do so.

Edwin Stanton, a close friend and member of Lincoln's cabinet, once confided that, "I have known that the president is not like other men, and that he believes that the future can be seen now and that the afterlife is for repentance. It would not surprise me if, when he dies, his spirit refused to leave the White House and that it remains there, restless and troubled, until it feels that the last of these 'sins' has been paid for."

Far-fetched and fanciful though this seemed, it began to make sense to Harry Truman some ninety years later as he pondered the mysterious spectral visitor outside the presidential bedroom doors. The more he read about Lincoln's alleged psychic abilities and the series of ghostly visions the late president claimed to have had while in the White House, the more convinced Truman became that Lincoln's tormented ghost still haunted the White House.

"It's possible," he said. "Anything's possible."

At first Truman attributed the incidents to his over-wrought imagination and the strain of office. The fact that the hauntings occurred at the outset of the Cold War suggested to him that the phantom president was trying to warn him about deteriorating East-West relations.

The idea seemed entirely possible to Truman. Somehow the ghost of the president who had fought so hard to preserve the Union in another time was trying to tell him something—perhaps to warn him about the ever-growing Communist threat and the apparent ambition of Russia to dominate the world.

To the end of his days—he died in 1972—Truman believed that whoever was president, and whoever lived in the White House, would also hear the discreet rappings on the bedroom doors and perhaps would someday have the opportunity to communicate directly with Lincoln's ghost.

So far, throughout subsequent administrations, no presidents have admitted to having encountered any ghostly manifestations, let alone having communicated with the troubled president from beyond the grave.

Does Ghost of Dead Banker Haunt Selma Mansion?

DEEP IN THE HEART OF SELMA, Alabama, there stands a handsome, multicolumned mansion that has been center stage for unexplained psychic phenomena ever since its owner was allegedly shot and killed by Yankee troops shortly after the end of the Civil War.

According to some town historians, the ghost of John Parkman still haunts the brooding old plantation home at 713 Mabry Street, which in recent years has become one of this town's most popular tourist spots.

Parkman was a twenty-nine-year-old banker, so the story goes, who had been thrown in jail by the occupying Federal forces for having illegally used bank funds to dabble in cotton speculation. He was shot trying to escape, according to the official record, even though some sources suggest he might have drowned in the Alabama River during the same escape attempt.

Whatever his fate, legend has it that his ghost has been seen numerous times wandering the many rooms of Sturtivant Hall, the neoclassically styled mansion built in 1853. Some witnesses claim to have also seen the spirits of his two dead daughters, their young faces pressed against the window late at night and occasionally in broad daylight.

One such witness is Betty Calloway, president of the Sturtivant Museum Association. At the time of the sighting, Mrs. Calloway lived across the street from the mansion.

"I saw the faces of two small girls, presumably the Parkman children, peering out an upstairs window," she said. Another time, she said, "We called the fire department because there was smoke coming out the window of that room, but the window was closed and they found no evidence of anything."

Another visitor, the commandant of a nearby Air Force base, also is alleged to have seen the two little girls at the window.

Azile Ellis, a museum guide, said she was alone in the house one day when she heard what sounded like footsteps on the second floor. "I was in the warming room. All of a sudden I could hear someone walking upstairs. It sounded like he had stopped at the head of the stairs, so I went to the stairs and looked up. There was no one there."

Ellis said the footsteps turned and went into another room where they continued for almost half an hour.

"I'm not one who goes bananas over ghosts, but there wasn't enough money to make me go up there and look," she said.

Perhaps the scariest encounter was related by Anne Davidson, a retired guide.

"One day a man came in to go through the house spraying for pests," she said. "He went upstairs, but in a few minutes he came hurriedly down. He was a newcomer in Selma, and he hadn't heard any of the stories. He said to me, 'Has anybody had any unpleasant experiences in that room at the head of the stairs?' He said someone or something had almost pushed him to the floor."

Other staff members and visitors have commented on doors opening and closing on their own, shutters flapping mysteriously, and strange moaning sounds coming from the second floor.

Roy Nix, a Selma police sergeant who lived in a small house behind the plantation, also had a run-in with something strange at Sturtivant Hall. "It was weird," he said. "I made rounds every night. It would be warm in a room, but suddenly it would go cold. Others have had this experience."

After Nix moved away, Troy Hughes, a medical supplies salesman, and his wife Camille rented the place. Ever since, they have been constantly awakened by alarm systems going off for no reason, doors opening and closing on their own, and shutters banging in the wind—even when locked from the inside.

"The only way you could open them would be from the inside of the house, and then you'd have to open the windows to get at the shutter latches," Hughes explained. "It's my responsibility to make sure the shutters are closed at night. But the shutters will be open in the morning."

One other episode convinced the Hugheses that some supernatural force had invaded the house.

"One time when we were out of town we came home and all the pictures on the wall were turned crooked," Hughes said. "A lot of things were moved around. The windows were sealed; there is no way anyone could have gotten in. We considered calling the police, but since nothing was missing we didn't do it."

Miracles and Visions

The Serpent's Kiss

ONE HOT SUMMER DAY in 1906, a devout young man named George Went Hensley had a vision while meditating on a lonely mountaintop overlooking his home near Grasshopper Valley, Tennessee.

In the vision, an angel came to him and told him that the surest way to salvation was to follow St. Mark's admonition to "take up serpents."

That afternoon Hensley wandered across the mountain until he found a rattlesnake sunning on a rocky ledge. Trembling, but resolute in his determination to stare Satan down, he picked up the snake and held it high.

Then he kissed it.

Convinced it was his faith that protected him, Hensley marched joyously down the mountain with his rattler. His first stop was at a local evangelical prayer meeting, where he feverishly related his revelation to friends and neighbors.

At first no one dared touch the poisonous viper. After repeated demonstrations, however, and readings from St. Mark, a few bold members reached out and fondled the snake. Instant jubilation exploded in the aisles as the hardscrabble assembly of dirt farmers, factory workers, and mill hands decided that God's power stood between them and the serpent's deadly fangs.

A new American religion had been born.

In the years that followed, hundreds of rural churchgoers converted to Hensley's unorthodox and dangerous form of worship. Snake-handling soon became a common practice at small churches, private homes, and woodland gatherings throughout eastern Tennessee.

By the 1930s, the use of rattlesnakes in church services had spread to several neighboring states. Virginia, West Virginia, Kentucky, the Carolinas, Georgia, Alabama, and Florida all reported snake-handling activities, usually in remote pockets far away from the ridicule of bigger churches and the long arm of the law.

In the early 1970s, for example, the sheriff of Berrien County, Georgia, told a local newspaper that the cult had a "wide number of followers" in his territory as well as in nearby counties. Sheriff Walter Gaskins recalled an instance in the mid-1960s when a local pastor had been tried for murder after a snake bit a worshipper.

In 1985, the pastor of a church in Cartersville, Georgia, died from the bite of a snake he had stroked during services. The pastor had refused medical treatment, believing until the end that the power of the Almighty would protect him from death.

At the pastor's funeral, mourning members of the congregation explained that "God's will has been done."

Over the years, at least fifty people have died either from snakebites or from the drinking of "salvation cocktails"—liquid laced with venom or strychnine—during religious ceremonies. It is not known how many other deaths and injuries have gone unreported.

This is because church leaders and members wisely keep their activities secret. Snake-handling is illegal in most states, and pastors are usually held accountable for the welfare of their congregation during ceremonies.

Still, snake-handling continues to flourish in out-of-the-way communities and hamlets, from Arkansas to Kentucky. Despite the danger of snakebites and of crackdowns by the law, this strange religious practice appears to be a favorite among some fundamentalist churches whose communicants believe the Holy Spirit confers supernatural gifts, such as the ability to speak in tongues and to heal by prayer, by the laying on of hands, and by anointing with oil.

Mainstream clergymen generally show little tolerance toward snake handlers, although opinions are mixed about where to draw the legal line between church and state. Most simply view the dangerous ritual as a "gross misinterpretation" of St. Mark's scripture.

"They [the cultists] have taken literal words and fashioned their own meaning from them," is how one Methodist minister in Georgia put it.

Another pastor in Alabama said: "God didn't intend for such sensationalism and foolishness to come into the church.... Handling snakes and drinking venom to express one's faith in Christ is ridiculous."

But handlers usually point to verses 17 and 18 in the last chapter of the Gospel of Mark as justification for their activity: "And these signs shall follow them that believe: In my name shall they cast out devils; they shall speak with new tongues; they shall take up serpents; and if they drink any deadly thing it shall not hurt them.... "

In 1965, fifty-nine years after founding his controversial religion, George Went Hensley was the guest speaker at a small, open-air service in Altha, Florida, when a small diamondback rattler draped across his arm bit him on the wrist.

"Nothing to worry about," the seventy-seven-year-old preacher assured the packed crowd. "It's just Satan knocking on the Lord's heavenly door."

The aging evangelist reminded the audience that snakebites were nothing new to him anyway. Over the past four decades, he figured he'd been bitten at least four hundred times.

But this time something seemed to be wrong.

A few minutes later, Hensley's skin turned purple and started swelling. Excruciating pain now racked his body and he found it hard to breathe. He lost his balance and stumbled to his knees.

Silence descended like a funeral shroud over the audience as they watched their leader struggle to regain his composure. Finally, a couple of men in the front row rushed to his aid.

But it was too late. The snake had struck hard, burying its tiny but lethal fangs into the preacher's veins and squeezing out a full load of venom.

The next morning George Went Hensley, "God's own anointed disciple of serpents," went into shock and died.

Mark Twain's Dream

MARK TWAIN, THE LITERARY father of Tom Sawyer and Huckleberry Finn, was a dreamer. In his dreams, his fevered mind rambled across unearthly landscapes, conjuring up unlikely heroes and demons.

Some of those dreams were brilliantly brought to life in the pages of his many books, essays, and letters.

But his eeriest dream—the one in which he "saw" his brother in a coffin the day before his death—is perhaps the most celebrated of all of the great writer's nightmarish encounters.

It all began when Twain, whose real name was Samuel Clemens, was working as a part-time riverboat pilot on the mighty Mississippi.

Twain loved the river. So did his younger brother, Henry, who begged the not-yet-famous author to help him get a job aboard the *Pennsylvania*, a sleek, multideck steamer that made frequent trips up and down the Mississippi from St. Louis to New Orleans.

Twain managed to get him a job as a "mud clerk." The pay was low, the hours were long and hard, and the glamour was non-existent. But Henry didn't care, as long as he was on the river with the brother he admired so much.

In St. Louis, they often stayed overnight with their sister Pamela, and her husband, William A. Moffett. It was at their home one cold and rainy night that Twain dreamed about Henry's death.

The vision came to him with such startling clarity that he awoke the next morning convinced that what he had seen in the dream was real. In his heart, he knew Henry was dead.

As he later recalled, he saw Henry, laid out in a metal coffin bridging two chairs in his sister's parlor in St. Louis. The corpse was dressed in one of Twain's old suits, and in his hands he clutched a bouquet of white and red roses. In the dream, his brother seemed to be at peace, though something told him he had died a horribly agonizing death.

Twain arose before breakfast and went for a walk, trying to shake loose from the horrifying dream. The image of his dead brother's face floated before his eyes. He could even smell the roses and the funeral balm as he strolled down first one street, then another, fearful that what he had seen was a grim reality.

A few minutes later he stopped. What am I doing to myself, he wondered. Henry's not dead! It was just a silly dream, a nightmare, nothing more.

Somewhat relieved, but still not convinced, he turned around and raced back toward the house. He went straight into the parlor, half expecting to see the shiny metal coffin with his brother's body stretched between two chairs.

Twain almost let out a whoop when he saw there was no coffin in the room.

Although the memory of the dream had faded to some degree by the next day, Twain still felt chilled whenever he thought about it. Perhaps it was his preoccupation with the dream that led to a disagreement between Twain and his captain. Whatever the cause, the despondent riverboat pilot was fired from his job aboard the *Pennsylvania*.

A few days later the big steamer, minus its outspoken writer-pilot, chugged out of New Orleans upriver toward St. Louis. Henry, happy to still have a job, was on board, still working as a mud clerk.

Everything was going fine until the boat drew within a few miles of Memphis. Suddenly, without warning, there was a deafening roar inside the dark and dirty engine room, followed by a colossal explosion. Hot sparks and metal flew everywhere, raining down on the river with a great hissing sound.

The ship literally blew apart, killing dozens of passengers and crewmen. Henry survived the blast and was carried to a makeshift hospital on the banks of the river. The outlook was bleak for the brother of America's most famous humorist: he had inhaled considerable quantities of scalding steam—so much, in fact, he wasn't expected to live through the night.

As fate would have it, Twain was on another steamer one day's journey behind the *Pennsylvania*. At several stops along the way, he picked up stories about the accident. With each retelling of the story, the news grew more grim.

Twain couldn't help remembering the disturbing dream of a few nights before. It flooded his mind, shoving aside all other thoughts. Desperately he hurried on up the river until he reached his brother's side.

Henry was alive, but just barely. Ironically, the attending physician told Twain his brother would be fine.

Then, sometime during the night, another doctor gave Henry an injection of morphine. Unfortunately, it was too much, and Henry died a few hours later.

Beth Scott and Michael Norman, authors of *Haunted Heartland,* have researched the case thoroughly. The following passage from their book, which describes the harrowing events that followed, is proof, say some, that Mark Twain was one of the most psychically gifted persons in American history:

"His [Henry's] body was carried into what was called the 'dead room' and placed in the only metal coffin available…. That is where Sam (Mark) found him. At once the dream came back to him in perfect detail. Henry was dressed in one of Sam's suits.

"As Sam stood near the casket, an elderly woman walked in and placed in the dead boy's hands a bouquet of roses. They were white … with a single red rose at the center."

Sometime later that day the Moffetts had Henry's body sent to their home to lie in state. It was there, in the Moffetts' parlor, that the final part of Twain's vision was rekindled.

"Sam raced ahead," wrote Scott and Norman, "wanting to save his mother the trauma of viewing Henry's morphine-twisted face. He arrived just in time to forestall the unloading while he went inside to comfort her. Upstairs in the sitting room, he found two chairs spaced a coffin's length apart, waiting to receive their burden."

Had he arrived a few minutes later the casket would have been positioned on them, the final detail of his dream fulfilled.

Miracle in the Clouds

ALL HER LIFE Francis Tippins had been a kind, caring woman who rarely complained about anything.

Her friendly smile was legendary.

"She was one of the happiest, brightest, and most cheerful persons I've ever known," a neighbor recalled. "She was like a saint—always doing things for the church, local school, and community, always smiling and never asking for anything in return."

When she retired from the Baxley, Georgia, school system, Mrs. Tippins remained active in her small south Georgia hometown, promoting community events and festivals and helping out the needy.

She never stopped.

Then one day she felt a sharp pain in her lower chest. When her husband, Dennard, offered to take her to a doctor, she declined, assuring him she'd be better in a few days.

The pain got worse.

Still, she refused to see a doctor—or to slow down. For months she courageously kept the pain to herself, not wishing to bother her busy husband, a prominent local businessman and farmer.

Finally, unable to endure the suffering any longer, she spoke up, and the alarmed Mr. Tippins got her to a doctor.

It was cancer.

"We were shocked," a friend related. "This brave woman had been suffering all these months, yet she went on about her business without anybody knowing, helping others and going to church. It was amazing."

The cancer continued to spread in spite of treatment at several regional hospitals. Doctors told Mr. Tippins there was nothing more they could do.

So it went for another dozen years. Some days the spirited ex-schoolteacher felt fine and looked forward to full recovery; at other times the pain became so intense that she had to be sedated.

Through it all, however, Francis Tippins continued to smile, never once complaining.

"That woman suffered so much," her friend noted. "God surely had a purpose for all that pain."

Although Dennard Tippins went to church, he was never one to believe in magic or miracles. But he prayed. For twelve long years he prayed that the disease sapping the life out of his beloved wife would go away, that she could get back on her feet and one day be whole again.

But, as he later admitted to friends, "God must have had other plans for Francis."

In the early 1980s Mrs. Tippins was hospitalized in Brunswick. Specialists worked around the clock to ease their saintly patient's suffering, but to no avail. As he watched and waited, Mr. Tippins knew the end was near.

To be closer to his wife, Mr. Tippins gave up his business and went to Brunswick. He bought a motor home which he kept parked in the hospital parking lot. By day he stayed by Mrs. Tippins side; by night he slept in the RV.

"He never left her side," a nurse recalled. "He stayed with her until the staff had to shoo him out to his RV at night."

Then one morning, as a gray and windswept sky hovered over Brunswick, Mr. Tippins was summoned to his wife's bedside. For several minutes he stood over his sick wife, listening to her final gasps for breath.

"I could see death all over her face," Mr. Tippins was later quoted as saying. "But there was no sadness in her eyes. Only a strange happiness."

About eleven o'clock in the morning, her condition deteriorated. At that point a nurse suggested that Mr. Tippins go out to his motor home and get some rest. Since there was nothing he could do—he had been by his wife's side for six straight hours, watching her graceful but futile struggle for life—the grieving husband agreed.

As he started across the parking lot, a light rain began to fall. Mr. Tippins had never felt so lonely, so sad, so utterly helpless. His lifelong companion—his wife and the mother of his children—was dying and there was not one thing he could do about it.

He went inside his motor home and prayed.

Sleep came softly, almost like an uninvited whisper. He dreamed he and his wife were back home, and they were young and she was well again. It was a sad, sweet dream and when he awoke to the rain, he was crying.

Outside a strong wind had picked up, gusting across the parking lot and blowing the rain about the lonely motor home. Then a strange thing happened—the rain suddenly stopped and the sun came out.

"It was raining and windy one second, then sunny and calm the next," Mr. Tippins recalled.

He sat up in bed, thankful for the calm.

That's when he heard the sound, a "whooshing, swishing" noise that sounded like the wind. He looked out the window. Not a leaf or branch was stirring.

That's odd, he thought, heading for the door. The whooshing, swishing sound continued.

He opened the door and looked outside.

His mouth dropped open.

Above the motor home, arching slowly across the sky toward him like a flaming meteor, was Francis.

"She was like an angel, flying overhead straight toward me," the astonished husband explained. "She had wings and there was a glow all around her. She was smiling."

Then, as suddenly as it had appeared, the apparition vanished.

"I knew what had happened," he said.

After collecting himself, Mr. Tippins walked over to the hospital. He saw the nurses standing outside his wife's door and walked straight toward them.

They told him his wife had just died.

Until his death in the late 1980s, Dennard Tippins continued to believe that he had witnessed a miracle that morning in Brunswick.

Coming Back from the Dead

ONE HOT HAZY AFTERNOON the early 1980s, a young Austin, Texas, man named Bob Smith crawled out onto his roof to install a new shortwave radio antenna he had just purchased.

As a broadcasting consultant, Smith had installed hundreds of radio and television antennae in his time. Still, he was aware of the danger and never took the job lightly.

On this particular day everything was going fine until a guy wire slipped. The antenna lurched to the right—not far, but just far enough to brush against a live power line.

Before he could move out of the way, seventy-two hundred volts of electrical energy surged through Smith's body, electrocuting him on the spot.

Then something strange happened.

"I came back to life," Smith said during an interview on a nationwide radio talk show. "First I was dead—I could see my body slumped over the roof, electrocuted. Then I was back, very much alive."

It had been over in a flash. One thing Smith recalled clearly from his ordeal was a profound sense of peace and harmony.

"There was a bright light coming toward me," he explained. "It was like a tunnel and it was as natural as sunlight coming in through my window. I felt glorious, completely at peace."

And he remembered one other thing.

"Even though I didn't understand what was happening to me at the time, I was aware that I had to make a choice— either to go on or return to life."

He chose to come back.

Apparently Smith had experienced what some scientists call a near-death-experience, or NDE. According to parapsychologists and others who study the phenomenon, tens of thousands of Americans experience near-death episodes every year. One source estimated that as many as twenty-three million people in the United States have died and come back to talk about their experience.

Many of these "survivors" were pronounced clinically dead, but revived to provide detailed—and often startling— accounts of leaving their body, passing into a light, and, in some cases at least, visiting "heavenly" realms.

P.M.H. Atwater, author of the best-selling book, *Coming Back to Life: The After-Effects of the Near-Death-Experience,* insists that NDEs occur frequently.

"It's been shown that forty percent of all resuscitated patients have near-death-experiences," said Atwater, a Charlottesville, Virginia, writer who claims to be an NDE survivor herself.

How does one know if he or she has had an NDE?

In her book, Atwater lists eight specific aspects of the phenomenon commonly described by survivors:

- Sensation of floating out of one's body
- Passing through a dark tunnel or black hole
- Ascending toward a light at the end of darkness
- Greetings from friendly voices, people, or beings
- Seeing a panoramic review of the life just lived from birth to death in reverse order
- Reluctance to return to the earthplane
- Warped sense of time and space
- Disappointment at being revived

"People all over the world, of different religions and different cultures, report the same basic phenomenon in much the same manner, even children," the author said. "Few episodes contain all of the eight elements. Most have about half; some, two or three."

Most survivors have trouble recalling how long they were "dead." Atwater, who has interviewed hundreds of people who claimed to have died and come back, said the average time is about five minutes, though some experiences last for more than an hour.

Bob Smith said he had no idea how long he was out. But it had to be "quite a while," he noted, because when he finally awoke he was in a hospital operating room.

When he related his experience to attending physicians they dismissed it as "hallucination ... brought on by the electrical shock."

Like most survivors, Smith said he rarely talks about his NDE anymore for fear of ridicule. In fact, he added, men are more reluctant to talk about their sensation than are women.

"Women usually speak out about this thing," Smith went on. "Why that's so, I haven't the faintest idea."

Atwater said the vast majority of survivors, regardless of the length of their NDE or their degree of involvement in the experience, commented about the "incredible, over-whelming love they felt, the peace, the feeling of total acceptance, and the presence of God."

She said survivors often relate how they encountered "beings of light" on the other side, while others saw beings who appeared to be human and wore either modern or old-fashioned clothes, or seemed "angel-like" in shape.

"Once you get there you feel a total, complete harmony with something superior," Smith pointed out. "It's a natural progression. There is no fear."

If NDEs are so common, then why isn't more known about them—and why don't more survivors come forth to talk about them?

"Old-fashioned fear of ridicule," quipped Smith. "That, plus the fact that most NDEs occur in hospital environments and medication somehow prevents most patients from remembering what happened to them."

Most survivors of NDEs are quick to point out they no longer fear death. Also, added Atwater, these people "usually become more loving, more peaceful, and much more content, with a less materialistic lifestyle."

At any rate, she said coming back from the dead need not be the nightmare most people dread.

"It can and should be an opportunity to enhance and enlarge our horizons, to relearn and redefine, to begin again," she said.

The Ghost Lights of Brown Mountain

GHOST LIGHTS ARE NOTHING NEW to the folklore of the South. Since Indian times, stories about mysterious flashing lights and wispy halos of color floating on the night wind have entertained and terrified generations of Southerners.

Nearly every county in every state has its own legend or two about ghost lights—or spook lights as they are frequently called—most of them associated with railroad lines and the spirits of railway workers who met untimely ends.

One of the most famous of these lights is seen from time to time near the small town of Maco in eastern North Carolina. Known as the Maco Light, it often appears suddenly on dark nights, bobbing and weaving beside a desolate stretch of railroad track before disappearing as suddenly as it arrived.

Locals claim the light has been around since 1869 when a train conductor named Joe Baldwin was decapitated in a freak accident. Some say the luminescent ball of light often seen in the vicinity of the tracks is the spirit of Baldwin, swinging a lantern as he searches for his severed head.

The Maco Light received nationwide publicity twenty years after the accident, when President Grover Cleveland reportedly witnessed the phenomenon during a stop-off at Maco Station. It was a hot summer night, so the story goes, and Cleveland had just stepped off the train to stretch his legs when he saw it—a strange white light, swirling and throbbing in the distance.

Thinking it was perhaps a signal from a brakeman or engineer, the president climbed back aboard. Later he asked a railroad employee about the strange light.

"What you've seen, sir, is the Maco ghost light," the employee responded.

In more recent times, critics have tried to debunk the Maco ghost light by claiming it is merely the reflection from auto headlights on nearby roads or highways. But there were no cars in 1869 when old Joe Baldwin lost his head and reports of the mysterious light were first recorded.

Another ghostly phenomenon that continues to astonish visitors to the western North Carolina mountains is the Brown Mountain Light. Usually visible on partly cloudy nights when the moon hangs low over northern Burke County, the light ranges in color from yellow to blood-red.

Many legends have cropped up about the light over the years, but the first documented sighting was in 1771 when a German engineer named William Gerard de Brahm visited the area. Brahm theorized that the light was nothing more than inflamed nitrous vapor carried by the wind—an explanation that has since turned out to be inaccurate.

Cherokee legends link the lights to the spirits of warriors killed in a great battle with the Catawba Indians at the base of Brown Mountain centuries ago.

Despite numerous scientific attempts to explain the eerie phenomenon, the Brown Mountain Light remains as mysterious today as it was during the great Indian clash. And, as with most spook lights, a significant body of folklore has sprung up around the apparition.

In 1913, a U.S. Geological Survey investigation verified that the light did indeed exist. After a brief examination, however, the investigators concluded that the light was nothing more than the reflected headlights of trains traveling through the Catawba Valley at the base of Brown Mountain—even though the spectacle had been seen long before the coming of trains to the valley!

Later that decade a team of scientists returned to Brown Mountain to put the legend to rest once and for all. Using a wide array of modern instruments, the scientists determined that lights appearing above the mountain arose from the spontaneous combustion of marsh gases.

The locals knew that couldn't be true either, for there simply weren't any marshy areas on or anywhere near Brown Mountain, nor any holes where such gases could gather.

A team of Smithsonian Institution investigators discounted the possibility that the lights were a manifestation of St. Elmo's Fire—an eerie, electric-glow phenomenon—because such conditions do not occur in mid-sky as do the Brown Mountain lights.

When all attempts at scientific explanations failed, folklore took over. Early lumberjacks working the area soon spread the story that the mysterious colored lights were the reflection of the moon off a rare gem somewhere on the mountain's face.

Fantastic Beasts

The Flintville Horror

FOR YEARS THE PEOPLE OF FLINTVILLE, Tennessee, a quiet little farming community nestled in the foothills of the Appalachians, have been bothered by a giant, hairy creature that seems to enjoy attacking automobiles and trying to snatch little children.

Locals call the creature "Bigfoot" because of the enormous footprints it leaves behind and because of its uncanny resemblance to the more famous behemoth many people believe inhabits remote regions of the Pacific Northwest.

Exactly what the Flintville monster is or where it came from remains a mystery, but more than two decades of sightings and terrifying encounters have left many people convinced that the creature is not only real but dangerous as well.

"That thing's so big it could easily hurt somebody," complained a local farmer who asked that his name not be used for fear of ridicule by outsiders. "Who knows how many head of our livestock have gone missing because of it?"

So far no one has been hurt by the Flintville monster, which often leaves behind sixteen-inch footprints along with a foul, "skunk-like" odor.

But there are those who claim to have had close calls, such as the man who insisted that a "seven-foot-tall hairy monster" chased him through the woods, howling and screeching at him like an ape, or the woman whose car was attacked by the same kind of creature while she hid on the floorboard.

On at least one occasion, a child was nearly kidnapped by a thing with long, hairy arms.

The trouble began in 1976, when a woman told police that a "giant, hairy monster" broke her automobile antenna and then jumped onto the roof of her car and began bouncing up and down. As soon as the woman's story made the headlines, other citizens stepped forth to describe similar encounters with Bigfoot-like beasts.

Of all the stories, however, none can match the nearly tragic drama related by Mrs. Jennie Roberston.

On April 26, 1976, Mrs. Robertson's four-year-old son Gary was outside playing in the yard when his mother heard him scream. It was late afternoon, Mrs. Robertson recalled, near sundown, and a cool afternoon breeze floated in from the woods across from her yard.

When she ran outside to investigate, she became conscious of a foul odor that reminded her of a skunk or "dead rats." Then she saw it—a huge, apelike figure loping around the corner of the house.

"It was seven or eight feet tall," she told investigators, "and seemed to be all covered with hair. It reached out its long, hairy arms toward Gary and came within a few inches of him."

Seconds before the shaggy beast encircled the child with its arms, however, the terrified mother snatched up her son, darted inside the house, and locked the doors. When she got up enough courage to look out the window, she saw a "big, black shape disappearing into the woods."

The first thing she did was pick up the phone and call her neighbor. Then she called the police. Within minutes, half a dozen men armed with shotguns and rifles surrounded her house, searching for clues to the mysterious animal's whereabouts.

One and all, they resolved to track down the brutish thing that had nearly captured little Gary Robertson. It was obviously the same creature that had been rampaging through the community for months, breaking automobile windshields, beating on the sides of houses, and filling the night air with bloodcurdling shrieks.

Throughout the night, relay teams of hunters combed the rugged woods on the outskirts of town, guns at the ready, eyes and ears keenly attuned to the shifting shadows and strange noises of the swamp. Several times they thought they heard the monster, grunting and snorting at them from behind bushes, and several times they opened fire.

With each onslaught of bullets, the monster would issue a high-pitched squeal. Instead of falling, however, the enraged beast threw rocks at its attackers before bounding away into the brush.

The next day the hunters found more sixteen-inch footprints in the ground, as well as hair, blood, and mucus. The hair was scientifically analyzed but could not be identified.

Throughout the South, from Arkansas to Virginia, reports of monsters resembling Bigfoot continue to trickle in across the desks of law enforcement officers and park rangers. The vast majority of these sightings can be dismissed as hoaxes, of course, or illusions triggered by poor visibility or unsteady imaginations.

But a few—like the Flintville monster—cannot be explained away so easily.

The Lair of the Beast

IN HIS BOOK, *Beast,* author Peter Benchley writes about a giant squid that terrorizes the waters around Bermuda, crushing boats and munching on hapless mariners at will until it finally runs into a pack of hungry sperm whales, the creature's only natural enemy.

After a titanic struggle, the beast—which had been forced up from the briny depths because of changing environmental conditions—is finally bested and its nautical reign of terror is over.

Although a work of fiction, Benchley's nightmarish creation is very real to the people of the Bahama Islands. For centuries Bahamian sailors have known of just such a sea beast. Some call it the *lusca*—a many-armed monster that emerges from the deep sea when hungry, roiling the waters with its enormous tentacles and dragging boats and their crews to the ocean floor.

Many old-timers believe there is no way to escape the monster's powerful coils and sharp teeth. An encounter with a lusca on the high seas means certain death.

The legendary lairs of the lusca are the mysterious "blue holes" of the Bahamas. Until recently, not much was known about these dark, blue pools, sometimes reaching hundreds of feet below the surface.

Island fishermen naturally assumed that these deep holes were home to the lusca, as well as to other horrors of the deep, and avoided them whenever possible.

Today we know the holes are actually subterranean caverns that were formed about eighteen thousand years ago when a giant continental icecap removed oceanic waters, lowering the level of the seas by hundreds of feet. At that time, the Bahama Islands were hills on a vast tropical plain. Rainwater, made acid by tropical vegetation, seeped into the soil, eroding and dissolving the limestone bedrock and creating vast undersea caverns.

Some of the caverns collapsed under the weight of the surface soil, becoming sinkholes of the sort that dot the Caribbean landscape and that of nearby Florida. When the ice melted, the seas rose and submerged the lowlands; the sinkholes became the blue holes that would later inspire such fear and fascination.

Although few scientists seriously believe the holes are inhabited by a giant squid, there are real dangers. For example, tidal flows trapped within the cavernous underwater passageways can create swift currents that churn the surface and form whirlpools capable of sucking small boats to the bottom.

Divers, too, are vulnerable to the strong currents. Usually the holes can be explored safely only twice a day, during the brief period when the tide is slack and the caverns' interiors are calm.

Once inside, divers find that the blue holes enclose a fantasy world of rock and marine life. Stalactites hang from cavern ceilings, relics of the time before the submergence; blind, colorless fish swim in their depths; lobsters and other crustaceans abound; and many species can be found nowhere else but in these marine caves.

To be sure, divers exploring the blue holes often encounter octopuses and squid. But these are hardly the terrifying creatures of legend. In fact, most are small, ranging from a few inches to slightly less than three feet in length, including tentacles.

Larger forms of these cephalopods (the name comes from Greek words meaning "head foot") do exist, however, and they can be quite terrifying—and dangerous—when startled.

Old salts up and down the eastern seaboard delight in telling and retelling stories about alarming encounters with these "many-armed" demons from the depths. To be ensnared in the squirming arms of a giant squid and dragged down to a watery grave remains a maritimer's greatest nightmare.

Although various forms of cephalopods have existed for the past five hundred million years, not much factual information is known about them. Given the abundance of these sea creatures around the world, that seems ironic.

One source lists more than 350 known species of giant squid, some of which have been reported to range up to one hundred feet in length. Measurements of scars taken from captured whales indicate that giant squids—also known as cuttlefish, calamary, devilfish, and the dreaded kraken of Scandinavian lore—occasionally attain lengths in excess of 120 feet!

The giant squid, like other members of the squid family, has a pair of highly developed eyes with a human look about them, a parrotlike beak and ten sucker-bearing arms. These arms, or tentacles, are rimmed with teeth capable of inflicting severe injuries to man or whale—the creature's only two enemies.

Marine experts such as James V. Sweeney insist that giant squid are among the most dangerous life forms in the sea. In his book, *A Pictorial History of Sea Monsters and Other Dangerous Marine Life,* Sweeney points out that squid "are known to be extremely dangerous when hooked [by fishermen] ... and quite risky to bring aboard if taken from a small boat."

Should the opportunity present itself, he added, "these mammoth-sized squid will bite, wreck small craft, or make off with a human."

Many stories still circulate among the islanders about chilling encounters with the lusca. Hardly a year goes by without at least one sighting, and whenever a fisherman is missing, it is said he has gone down to the lair of the beast.

Of Rain Gods and Fish-Men

OUT OF THE HISTORICAL twilight zone of precolonial America, there has emerged a collection of myths, legends, miracles, and mysteries that have intrigued and entertained generations of scholars.

Today it might seem incredible to think that some scientists and historians once accepted as fact many of these fantastic fables. But accept them they did, sometimes even exaggerating and embellishing bizarre accounts of New World adventures and discoveries to suit their own whim or enhance their own fortune.

The prevalence of such far-out fantasies no doubt added spice to the world of Renaissance man. But it also stalled serious scientific and historical inquiry for centuries.

For more than a hundred years after the Europeans first set foot on New World shores, marvelous tales about shining cities, lost treasures, wondrous races, and intriguing phenomena were circulated in every maritime country of Europe. Since Spain was the acknowledged first nation to plant colonies in the Western Hemisphere, the task of recording these strange events naturally fell to Spanish historians.

Like Herodotus, whom they greatly admired, Spanish historians wrote prolifically about everything. Florida, which comprised roughly the entire Southeast, had no small role in the "Northern Mystery," and was the setting for an amazing number of supernatural and fanciful episodes. To be sure, what may have been simple and not unusual occurrences often became miracles after a few embellished recountings; and as Spanish explorers pushed deeper into the wilderness their chronicles grew wilder and wilder.

Following are a couple of the most popular stories first told by clerical historians. It should be remembered that each was given wide credence by the readers of that day.

On April 4, 1566, a party of Spaniards under the leadership of Governor Menendez de Aviles landed at St. Catherine's Island off the coast of Georgia. At that time the region was in the throes of a severe drought which threatened to ruin the corn and bean crops.

The natives were desperate. A group of Guale Indians had already sacrificed several victims in an unsuccessful attempt to secure aid from the rain gods. Undoubtedly there would have been more human sacrifices had the Spanish leader himself not intervened.

A group of chiefs approached Menendez and asked him for help. It was their wish that he command the god of the Spaniards to send rain, but the powerful Spanish leader declined because the Indians were heathens.

At that point, a couple of Menendez's young soldiers decided to secretly intervene. Thinking to indulge in a practical joke at the expense of the distressed Indians, the soldiers—both teenagers—informed them through an interpreter that they would ask their god for rain.

The savages were naturally delighted and heaped gifts of fish, corn, and deerskins upon the soldiers. Instead of helping them, however, the young Spaniards took the goods and departed to gloat over the success of their scheme.

When the story reached Menendez, he had the soldiers stripped in preparation for flogging. At the last second, an old Indian chief intervened on behalf of the youths.

"You have deceived me," he said, "for you will not ask God for rain, and now you wish to punish the children because they are willing to pray for it. Do not whip them, for I no longer wish them to pray for water, and am content that it will rain when God wills it."

Menendez then informed the Indian leader that if he would convert to Christianity, he would call on its great god to bring rain. The chief walked straight to the cross, kneeled before it, and cried out, "Behold, I am a Christian!"

According to the chronicler of the incident, "this occurred at two o'clock in the afternoon. Half an hour later it began to thunder and lighten and to rain with such violence that it did not cease for twenty-four hours, and extended in a circuit of five leagues."

Within a month, Menendez appeared again in the role of glorified rainmaker. This time he had sailed twenty leagues up the St. John's River and was approaching a village ruled over by the powerful chieftain, Outina.

Six Spaniards were sent ahead to the village to announce the approach of the visitors. Outina replied by inviting Menendez to enter the town with twenty of his men and to beseech God to send rain upon the famished crops.

The commander concealed his amusement and entered the presence of the Indians. Immediately it began to rain and the natives fled in terror from one whose influence was so powerful.

Another story that tickled the fancies of many Europeans was that of the "fish-men of Inzignanin." According to Peter Martyr, there lived near Chicora—an area between North and South Carolina—a quaint race of men and women who had scales and webbed hands.

Most incredible were their tails, described as "half a meter long and thick as a man's arm."

The tails were not movable but formed one mass, much like those of crocodiles and alligators. When these men wished to sit down, they had to have a seat with an open bottom; and if no suitable seat was available, they had to dig a hole more than a cubit deep in which to accommodate their long posteriors.

These curious people ate nothing but raw fish. According to Martyr, "when the fish gave out, they all perished, leaving no descendants ...."

The White River and Galveston Monsters

CLOYCE WARREN OF NEWPORT, Arkansas, thought he was seeing things one spring morning in 1971 when he and two fishing companions noticed a strange disturbance in the murky waters of the White River, a few yards from their small boat.

The trio had just cast their lines not far from the White River Bridge and were settling back for a relaxing day on the water, when suddenly the calm surface was broken by a huge column of water spewing skyward.

"I didn't know what the heck was happening," Warren, an employee with the White River Lumber Company, told reporters.

Seconds later, a giant serpentine form rose above the waves and began moving in the middle of the river, away from the boat. Warren described the creature as "long and gray colored ... with a spiny backbone that stretched for more than thirty feet."

Before the monster sank beneath the surface and disappeared, Warren snapped a picture of it with the Polaroid camera he had brought along that morning to photograph their day's catch. The creature in the picture, which was published in the *Newport Daily Independent* two days later, was billed as the White River Monster.

For years, fishermen and boaters along the White River have told hair-raising stories about encounters with some kind of large, aquatic creature which, in time, the locals also nicknamed the White River Monster. Skeptics—and there are many—theorize that the "monster" is nothing more than elephant seals that occasionally stray up the Mississippi and into the White River.

According to experts, most sightings of strange creatures, both in inland waters and at sea, can be attributed to mistaken identity—seaweed, floating logs, schools of fish, or a number of other simple explanations. Sometimes even unexpected ripples in water caused by the wind are enough to give veteran mariners the heebie-jeebies.

Less clearly explained, however, was the seventy-foot-long creature seen undulating through the waves off the coast of Galveston, Texas, in the late spring of 1872. This time, the entire crew of the *Saint Olaf*, A Norwegian-registered bark with twenty men aboard, laid eyes on a nightmarish behemoth that had horns, fins, and a long, pointed tail.

The *Saint Olaf's* captain, Alfred Hassel, issued the following signed statement about the Galveston monster:

"On a nearer approach we saw that it was an immense serpent, with its head out of the water ... about 200 feet from the vessel. He [the serpent] lay still on the surface at first ... lifting his head up, and moving the body in a serpentine manner. Could not see all of it; but what we could see, from the after part of the head, was about 70 feet long and of the same thickness all the way, excepting about the head and neck, which were smaller, and the former flat, like the head of a serpent...."

Hassel said the creature had "four fins on the back, and the body of a yellow greenish color, with brown spots all over the upper part and underneath white."

In his sworn statement, Hassel also said the creature was about six-feet in diameter, and that the waves "pushed out loudly" from its undulating motion.

The startled men of the *Saint Olaf* watched the creature for a full ten minutes before it finally sank beneath the waves and disappeared. One sailor thought he saw it resurface some time later, but no one was sure. The Galveston monster had simply vanished, like so many others reportedly spotted in the vicinity over the years.

Skeptics were quick to dismiss the sighting as nothing more than a long string of seaweed. In the fading afternoon sunlight, they reasoned, floating strands of weed rising and falling with the action of the waves could have easily been mistaken for a giant serpent.

Others suspected the creature might have been a school of porpoises or even sharks.

Some experts theorized it might even have been a serpent—a giant boa constrictor or some other kind of large snake that had perhaps drifted across the Gulf from Central America.

But seventy feet long? The longest serpent ever known in the New World—the anaconda—rarely exceeds twenty feet in length, though forty-footers have been reported.

It is also doubtful that any kind of land snake could have survived such a long voyage across the shark-infested Gulf.

What was the Galveston monster? Like Nessie, Chessie, Ogopogo, the White River Monster, and dozens of other strange sightings reported every year, the truth will probably never be known.

Unearthly Encounters

The Creatures Walk among Us

ON THE AFTERNOON OF October 11, 1973, two Mississippi men walked into the Pascagoula sheriff's office and claimed they had been captured by "robotlike" creatures from an unidentified flying object.

The bizarre incident had occurred while the two men, Calvin Parker and Charles Hickson, had been fishing on a secluded part of the Pascagoula River. The terrified fishermen said their ordeal began when a "bright, twenty-foot-long oval object" landed near them along the riverbank.

A few minutes later three strange creatures emerged from the UFO and started walking toward them.

Even though their first instinct was to run, "something held us," Parker later told newspaper reporters. "Those things wouldn't let us get away."

The men described the creatures as about five feet tall, with pale gray, "horribly wrinkled" skin. Hickson said, "They had no neck ... their arms ended in clawlike hands with only two fingers ... and their legs seemed to be fused together."

Parker fainted on the spot.

Under oath in the sheriff's office, Hickson swore he was carried off by one of the creatures while another managed to move his unconscious companion by beaming a ray at him that caused him to "float" toward the UFO.

The next thing he knew, Hickson said he was in a "very bright" room where a large, "eyelike" device "examined" him minutely. Some time later—neither man knew how long—they were "floated" out of the spacecraft and deposited on the riverbank.

When they came to later, the UFO was gone.

Parker said the first thing they did was go into town and have a couple of drinks. Then they decided to tell the sheriff. Hickson suspected the creatures might be planning to come back—perhaps launch an "invasion."

When a local newspaper reporter learned about the incident it became headline news. The two fishermen soon found themselves being interviewed by newspapers and television stations from as far away as New York City.

They had certainly hit the big time, but it wasn't what either man wanted. In the months to come both men complained of nightmares in which they saw the creatures again, and each time it appeared that the monstrous aliens were coming after them.

Were they telling the truth?

Lie detector tests supposedly corroborated their account. When a second test was proposed, however, Hickson refused. He said he'd had enough and just wanted to forget the whole thing.

Several investigators offered to hypnotize the men to see if they could uncover additional details about their harrowing ordeal. Both men refused, however, saying they were afraid of remembering too much.

But some UFO researchers say certain aspects about the fishermen's ordeal were similar to dozens of others happening all across the country at the time. In fact, the month of October 1973 is regarded by many UFO watchers as the busiest on record in the South.

Sightings of strange objects and even stranger creatures were cropping up in Florida, Texas, Virginia, Alabama, Georgia, South Carolina, North Carolina, Tennessee, Arkansas, and elsewhere in Mississippi. Some witnesses told of harrowing encounters with bizarre, bug-eyed aliens with "crablike" claws who enjoyed hauling captives off for examination aboard futuristic spaceships.

In Tanner Williams, Alabama, for example, a three-year-old boy told his mother he had been playing with a "nice monster" with "gray, wrinkled skin and pointed ears."

Had it not been for the Mississippi incident later that same day on October 11, no one would have thought twice about the boy's story of his strange "playmate."

Four days later, on October 15, a cab driver traveling on Interstate 90 between Gulfport and Biloxi claimed that his cab was immobilized by a blue UFO that landed in front of him. According to a newspaper report, the man was then approached by a creature with "crablike" claws and two shiny spots.

A similar creature reportedly was caught on film by Falkville, Alabama, police chief Jeff Greenhaw. The officer said he photographed a "being" in a silvery suit after he was called to the area to check on a UFO report.

Another "abduction" reportedly occurred that same month in Loxley, Georgia. Clarence Patterson said his pickup truck was "sucked" into a large cigar-shaped spacecraft where he was examined by several "robotlike creatures" who seemed to read his mind.

Other reports of alleged contact with alien beings continued to flood law enforcement agencies throughout the South. Near Chatham, Virginia, two teenagers said they were chased through the woods by a four-foot-tall "white thing" that ran sideways. The story coincided with several other reports about UFO landings in the area.

On October 19, an Ashburn, Georgia, woman said her car stalled when a strange object buzzed her from overhead. When she got out of her car to check the engine, she said a small man in metallic clothes approached her from the woods.

"He didn't bother me," the woman told reporters. "He just walked around the car, as if examining it, then went away, just disappeared."

The woman described the creature she saw as "short ... with some kind of bubble head and rectangular eyes."

While UFO reports continued that month in other parts of the country, the last reported "contact" occurred in Copeland, North Carolina, when a farm couple heard a loud whooshing noise outside their rural home. When they went outside to investigate, they saw a "small humanoid" form, dressed in what appeared to be a gold jumpsuit, walking across their yard.

When the creature saw them, it jumped back into the spacecraft and took off.

Falling Terrors

LATE ONE NIGHT in the summer of 1954, Mrs. Hewlett Hodges of Sylacauga, Alabama, was lying on her sofa listening to the radio when suddenly a large metallic ball crashed through the roof, bounced off a table, and struck her leg.

The startled woman would later recall that the strange object, which weighed about ten pounds, was "hot and smoking" when it finally came to rest in a corner of her living room floor.

Except for some frayed nerves and a bruised leg, the elderly woman walked away from her distressful brush with the unknown relatively unscathed.

Although she didn't know it at the time, Mrs. Hodges had just become the first person in modern times to be struck by a falling star—or, more precisely, a meteorite.

Even though unverified accounts of individuals being hit by falling stars exist in nearly every country, scientists say the odds of being hit by a meteorite are infinitesimally small—about one in ten billion. Historically speaking, there is only one report, unsubstantiated, of a person being killed by a hurtling object from space—an unfortunate Italian monk in 1650.

To date, however, there have been no confirmed fatalities.

That seems remarkable considering the fact that billions of meteorites swarm into the earth's atmosphere every day. Fortunately for humans, very few actually reach the ground. Nearly all, traveling at speeds fifty times faster than a high-powered rifle bullet, disintegrate into powder long before impact.

Meteorites falling from the sky are not the only celestial objects to arouse concern and speculation among earthlings. Down through the ages, stories of other spectacular skyfalls have thrilled and terrified more than a few witnesses.

In many parts of the world, frogs and toads have also fallen numerous times and in monstrous numbers; so have worms, mice, snakes, bite-sized bits of meat, beans, blood, spiders, squirrels, fish, hot stones, and even cats and dogs.

Such phenomena have often been attributed to freak whirlwinds, storms, and other natural occurrences. But not always. All too often mysterious skyfalls occur whenever there are no high winds, no storm, no other natural explanation.

Such was the case in 1877, when thousands of snakes fell from crystal-clear skies over Memphis, Tennessee. At first investigators blamed the strange skyfall on winds kicked up by a hurricane off the coast, but they later dismissed the idea. No one knew why the snakes—and nothing else—had been dropped on the city in such abundance.

Equally strange was the shower of warm stones that fell outside the offices of the *Charleston News & Courier* in Charleston, South Carolina, on September 4, 1886. The shower of stones—which struck twice within a five-hour period—shattered windows and pulverized the pavement outside the newspaper building.

Several times during the winter of 1891, residents of Valley Bend, West Virginia, found millions of unidentified white worms covering the snow. Where had the curious creatures come from? Nobody had a clue. The most widely held theory was that they had somehow fallen from the sky. Some people actually claimed to have seen them raining down out of the clouds.

Over the past century there have been many other baffling skyfalls in the South. Following are some of the most mysterious:

- March 21, 1889—A "sulphur rain" descended on Mount Vernon, Kentucky. The substance that fell was described as highly flammable.
- May 11, 1894—A gopher turtle encased in ice fell near Vicksburg, Mississippi, during a storm. Before conditions abated, it was reported that a small block of alabaster, also encased in ice, had fallen on Vicksburg itself.
- November 21, 1898—Spiders and spiderwebs dropped from the skies over Montgomery, Alabama. Some of the spiderwebs were described as several inches in diameter.
- June, 1901—Charles Raley, a cotton planter in South Carolina, was startled when hundreds of small catfish, trout, and perch suddenly started pouring down from the skies over his plantation. Workers later discovered freshly-fallen fish swimming in pools that had accumulated between the rows of cotton.
- October 23, 1947—The town of Marksville, Louisiana, was inundated by a deluge of fish—largemouth bass, sunfish, hickory shad, and minnows. Most of the fish were described as "absolutely fresh and fit for human consumption." Some were said to be frozen.
- November, 1958—Rain fell for almost three straight hours onto a ten-foot-square area of the home of Mrs. R. Babington in Alexandria, Louisiana. Local weather officials had no explanations for the strange deluge.
- July 12, 1961—Construction workers in Shreveport, Louisiana, had to take shelter when green peaches started raining down on them from a thick cloud. No whirlwinds, tornadoes, or other high winds were reported in the area at the time. One possible explanation: an airplane flying overhead somehow lost a cargo of unripened peaches!

The Demon Lights of the Swamp

LATE ONE AFTERNOON in the autumn of 1965, a ten-year-old boy was peddling his new bike down a twisting mountain road in North Carolina when, suddenly, a ball of fire "as big as a basketball" whooshed by, nearly knocking him off balance.

Startled, the boy watched as the strange fireball stopped, circled around, and came back toward him.

When the mysterious light flashed by him again—this time grazing his arm—the youngster jumped off his bike and fled on foot. He didn't stop running until he was safely behind the doors of his home three miles away.

What was the blazing, basketball-shaped object that terrorized the young mountain boy on that cool October evening?

Nobody can say for sure, but some experts suspect it was a form of ball lightning, a rare, natural phenomenon that has astonished and bewildered thousands of observers over the years.

For centuries, scientists have debated the existence of ball lightning. Until recently the eerie phenomenon was placed in the same category of folklore as ghosts, wampus cats, and spook lights.

In some regions of the rural South, ball lightning is still often confused with various other cracker-barrel phenomena known to folklorists as Jack-o'-the-lantern, will-o'-the-wisp, marsh gas, fox fire, and *ignis fatuus,* or foolish fire. Seen on a lonely back road after dark or in a swamp after a thunderstorm, these weird manifestations—believed to be caused by gases escaping from decaying timber—can be as beautiful as they are startling.

During slave days, a popular Negro legend was that of Jack-o'-the-lantern, a hairy goblin with goggle eyes and a huge mouth that haunted the swamps and fields surrounding the plantation. Often seen in marshy places at night, the sinister ball of light seemed to recede and then vanish before reappearing again.

One rumor—possibly of Irish origin but taken over by Delta slaves—had it that the Jack-o'-the-lantern was the wandering soul of a person who had been refused admittance to both heaven and hell. Others said he was the spirit of someone they knew, recently deceased.

Unlike marsh gas, however, which almost always appears bluish white and hazy, ball lightning may be red, orange, blue, or white, and is said to vary in size from that of grapes to basketballs. According to some accounts, contact with the balls is lethal, while others maintain that lightning balls are completely harmless.

Some investigators are quick to dismiss ball lightning as an optical illusion formed by the eye itself after seeing a dazzling discharge of ordinary lightning.

To be sure, most sightings of ball lightning occur outdoors, usually during or immediately following a thunderstorm. But there are many reports of luminous spheres matching the description of ball lightning occurring in enclosed spaces such as houses, barns, apartments, automobiles, and even airplane cabins.

Such was the case in January 1984, when the pilots of a Soviet Ilyushin-18 aircraft flying over the Black Sea saw a glowing fireball about four inches in diameter floating inside their airplane. On March 19, 1963, an eight-inch globe of ball lightning—about as bright as a ten-watt bulb and giving off no perceptible heat—emerged from the pilot's cabin and floated down the aisle of an airliner on a New York-to-Washington flight.

Assuming that ball lightning does exist, as most scientists do, two questions naturally arise: just what is it, and is it dangerous?

Many believers contend it is nothing more than an abnormal display of lightning. Normal lightning is an instantaneous electrical discharge between oppositely charged particles of matter, and is easily understood in terms of ordinary physical principles.

But lightning balls that persist for several seconds without any apparent means of "striking" between oppositely charged poles are much more difficult to explain. Such balls of fire can reach circumferences of ten inches in diameter and last about five full seconds before sometimes exploding with a bang.

Occasionally, ball lightning seems to leave a pungent smell. In about a quarter of the cases there is damage—broken windows, for example, or scorched grass—but rarely are humans injured by the phenomenon itself.

One woman in Florida who had been plagued by the mysterious fireballs once used a fly swatter to attack a basketball-sized sphere that had rolled into her kitchen!

Soviet scientist Pyotr Kapitsa, winner of the 1978 Nobel Prize in physics, recently suggested that the luminous spheres consisted of plasma—electrically charged atoms of gas—that are stimulated by natural radio waves to emit light.

Laboratory experiments by Japanese and Dutch scientists appear to substantiate this view, although some experts insist that the precise nature of ball lightning remains a mystery.

In an interview with *The New York Times*, Dr. Stanley Singer of Pasadena, Calif., chairman of the International Committee for Ball Lightning Research, said few if any scientists doubted the existence of ball lightning anymore, but he admitted that the phenomenon is "extremely rare."

If ball lightning does consist of plasma, as many scientists believe, it remains to be shown what force or forces hold the plasma together in spherical form, Singer said.

He suggested that some interference by reflected microwaves might be behind the phenomenon. But this explanation requires the existence of natural microwaves—a mysterious phenomenon that is yet to be proven itself.

Outrageous Coincidences

IT WAS A HOT SUMMER NIGHT in the mid-1930s. Allan Falby, captain of the El Paso (Texas) County Highway Patrol, was putting in a few extra hours at the office when word came in that a pickup truck was speeding through a nearby rural area.

Dutifully, the veteran lawman put aside his paperwork, hopped onto his motorcycle, and roared off after the truck. A few minutes later, he caught up with the speeding vehicle and, after switching on his siren, motioned for the driver to pull over.

Instead of obeying the officer, however, the driver of the truck shifted gears and sped away. Falby had no choice but to pursue—even though it was dark and the winding highway was slick from a light rain that had fallen earlier that day.

With siren wailing and light flashing, the captain gradually gained on the speeding truck. Then, as Falby drew within a few yards of its taillights, the driver of the pickup suddenly slammed on his brakes.

The lawman didn't have a chance. The motorcycle skidded first on the wet highway, then rammed full-speed into the rear of the truck. The collision threw Falby head over heels away from his mangled motorcycle—but not before his leg was split open by a jagged piece of metal.

For several minutes, he lay alone in the dark, blood gushing from a ruptured artery in his right leg. He would have died on the spot had it not been for the arrival of Alfred

Smith, a resident of El Paso County. Working quickly, Smith applied a tourniquet to Falby's wound. The tourniquet held until an ambulance arrived and whisked the injured officer to a hospital.

After several months, Falby regained use of his injured leg and was able to return to work.

The story didn't end there, however.

Five years later, Captain Allan Falby happened to be working the night shift again when he was summoned to a bad accident out on U.S. 80. The caller at the scene said an automobile had crashed into a tree, and that the driver appeared to be in critical condition.

Falby responded immediately, this time taking a car instead of a motorcycle. Minutes later, he was at the scene, pushing his way through a crowd of anxious onlookers.

Inside the wrecked car he found an unconscious man, his right leg bleeding badly from a ruptured artery. Falby pulled the motorist free of the wreckage and quickly applied a tourniquet to his wound.

Something about the unconscious stranger looked familiar to Falby. Several seconds passed before he realized the man was Alfred Smith—the same Alfred Smith who had saved his life five years earlier!

"It all goes to prove," Falby was later quoted as saying, "that one good tourniquet deserves another."

Was the second eerie encounter between Falby and Smith just coincidence—or something else?

For centuries, scientists, philosophers and other thinkers have argued that some unknown force, perhaps psychically controlled, is behind such bewildering encounters. In a treatise written in 1960, Carl Gustav Jung, one of the founders of twentieth-century psychology, called the force "synchronicity."

Colin Wilson, noted author and lecturer on the occult, describes synchronicity as "those baffling, apparently meaningful coincidences that give us the feeling that fate is trying to tell us something."

But he says it is important to distinguish between ordinary coincidences and synchronicity, which he defines as "a coincidence so outrageous that it cannot be shrugged off as coincidence."

Wilson said odd coincidences, such as happened to Captain Falby and Smith, "certainly produce in us the creepy feeling that fate is nudging us in the ribs, attempting to make us realize that life is more meaningful than we thought."

One of the most remarkable recent cases involving synchronicity happened to a friend of Dr. Warren Weaver, an American mathematician and expert on probability. As Weaver tells it, George D. Bryson of St. Louis was on his way to New York on a business trip when his train stopped in Louisville, Kentucky.

Since it was an overnight stop, Bryson decided to check into a nearby motel and then spend the evening sightseeing. A few minutes later, he found himself standing at the desk of the Brown Hotel preparing to register.

Jokingly, he asked if there was any mail for him.

"Yes, sir," the young receptionist replied, calmly handing him a letter addressed to Mr. George D. Bryson, Brown Hotel, Room 307.

"It turned out that the preceding resident of Room 307 was another George D. Bryson, an insurance executive from Montreal. "The two Mr. Brysons eventually met, so each could pinch the other to be sure he was real."

Wilson believes a better understanding of synchronicity could "make us aware that our power to change the world is far greater than we imagine."

Did Fate Link the Destinies of Lincoln and Kennedy?

ON THE DAY HE WAS ASSASSINATED, President Abraham Lincoln drew his security guard, William H. Cook, aside and said, "I believe there are men who want to take my life ... and I have no doubt they will do it."

A few seconds later the president added, "If it is to be done, it is impossible to prevent it."

Almost one hundred years later, John F. Kennedy remarked to his wife, Jackie, and his personal adviser, Ken O'Donnell, "If somebody wants to shoot me from a window with a rifle, nobody can stop it, so why worry about it?"

Kennedy's chilling comments were uttered on the morning of November 22, 1963. A few hours later the president would be dead, shot by a rifle fired from a window in Dallas.

Did Lincoln and Kennedy, two of the most popular presidents in American history, somehow share a bond in their premonitions of impending death?

For years, scholars have debated this and other intriguing questions about the bizarre Lincoln–Kennedy similarities. While answers remain as elusive today as they were in the aftermath of the Kennedy assassination, some experts point to a variety of startling coincidences that appear to link the two ill-fated chief executives.

Following are a few of the intriguing parallels between the pair of tragic assassinations:

- Lincoln was first elected to Congress in 1846. John Kennedy followed exactly one hundred years later—in 1946.
- Lincoln was elected as the sixteenth president of the United States on November 6, 1860. Kennedy was elected to be the country's thirty-fifth president on November 8, 1960—one hundred years later.
- After their deaths, both were succeeded by Southerners named Johnson. Andrew Johnson was born in 1808, and Lyndon Johnson in 1908.
- John Wilkes Booth, the man who killed Lincoln, was born in 1838, while Lee Harvey Oswald, Kennedy's killer, was born one hundred years later.
- Both assassins were Southerners, and both were shot before they could come to trial.
- Booth committed his crime in a theater and then ran to a barn. Oswald pulled the trigger on Kennedy from the window of a barnlike warehouse—and ran to a theater.
- Lincoln was killed in Ford's Theater. Kennedy met his death while riding in a Lincoln convertible made by the Ford Motor Company.
- Both Lincoln and Kennedy were deeply involved in civil rights issues.
- They were also both shot on a Friday in the presence of their wives.
- Both men were killed by a bullet that entered the head from behind.
- The first name of Lincoln's private secretary was John, the last name of Kennedy's private secretary was Lincoln.
- The names Lincoln and Kennedy each have seven letters.

- The names Andrew Johnson and Lyndon Johnson each have thirteen letters.
- The names John Wilkes Booth and Lee Harvey Oswald each have fifteen letters.

Another irony involving Kennedy concerns the so-called "Kennedy assassination [dollar] bill," issued in Dallas only two weeks before JFK was killed there.

Since Dallas is the location of the eleventh of the twelve Federal Reserve bank districts, the bill bears the letter K, the eleventh letter of the alphabet, and the numeral 11 appears in each corner. The serial number begins with K and ends with A, standing for "Kennedy Assassination."

Eleven also stands for November, the eleventh month of the year; two elevens equal twenty-two, the date of the tragedy. And the series number is 1963, the year the assassination occurred!

The Mysterious Airship

ON MARCH 29, 1897, Robert Hubbard of Sioux City, Iowa, was nearly killed when a mysterious aerial object with "glowing red lights" snatched him from his bicycle and dragged him along the ground for several hundred feet.

When Hubbard's ordeal—which occurred six years before Orville and Wilbur Wright's successful flight at Kitty Hawk—was reported in the national press, it caused quite a stir. The result was a rash of similar incidents involving strange aircraft that filled newspapers for weeks to come.

On April 1, for example, three days after the Hubbard story broke, hundreds of people in Kansas City, Kansas, watched spellbound while a brightly lit, cigar-shaped airship hovered over the city. According to local accounts, wierd voices and crackling noises were heard emanating from the strange craft.

Throughout the month of April, tens of thousands of Americans from California and Texas to Alabama and West Virginia told of terrifying encounters with "great airships" piloted by occupants "not of this earth." In nearly every case, the airship was described as "cigar-shaped" with beams of glowing red lights fanning out underneath.

One of the strangest stories came from Le Roy, Kansas. On the morning of April 21, farmer Alexander Hamilton was awakened by a strange, whirring sound out in the pasture. Thinking his cattle might be in trouble, Hamilton raced outside only to discover a "glowing, strange-shaped craft" trying to steal a cow by hoisting it up with a rope.

Earlier, on April 14, a series of landings was reported in Iowa. The *Cedar Rapids Evening Gazette* reported that a "giant, cigar-shaped" object landed on Union Station in the "wee morning" hours and that several local citizens were taken on board.

The next day, a similar object "came to rest" on the Waterloo, Iowa, fairgrounds, according to the local newspaper. While dozens of curious onlookers gawked, one of the vessel's occupants reportedly went to the police station to seek protection from the crowd.

Several sightings were reported on April 16. Two men from Rhome, Texas, said they saw a giant cigar heading west at 150 miles per hour. The same day, the *Fort Worth Register* reported that a man traveling near Cisco, Texas, saw an airship crash into a field.

According to the *Register,* several local citizens helped repair the downed aircraft, then watched it roar away.

In Paris, Texas, a night watchman said he saw a cigar-shaped craft that measured two hundred feet in length and had several large wings. Later, in Farmersville, Texas, several people said they heard the crew of an airship singing hymns.

Another bizarre encounter in Texas occurred on April 17, when a large airship came in low and buzzed the town of Aurora. The ship then continued north, where it finally struck a windmill on the farm of a Judge Procter and exploded.

People rushed to the scene of the crash and discovered the badly-mangled body of the pilot.

"He was not of this earth," said T.J. Weems, a Signal Corps officer who offered the astonishing speculation that the dead pilot was a Martian.

The next day the "Martian" was given a Christian burial.

On April 19, other airships were spotted near Sisterville, West Virginia, and El Paso, Texas. On both occasions multicolored lights flashed from portholes and strange voices were heard talking inside the ships.

Stories about the mysterious aircraft continued unabated in the months to come, as newspapers competed to come up with the wildest accounts. Then, as suddenly and mysteriously as they had appeared, the airships disappeared.

The airship commotion was forgotten until the 1960s, when researchers interested in UFOs began rummaging through old newspapers and came up with the original stories.

What were the airships? Where did they come from? Even today, investigators aren't really sure, though early rumors linked them to an unknown scientist involved with secret aircraft testing.

There is good reason to suspect that some of the stories were deliberate hoaxes, spread by overimaginative telegraph operators who reported many of the sightings, as well as by newspaper reporters themselves.

Friendly Angels from Beyond

FOR YEARS, A PRINCETON-EDUCATED theologian and Presbyterian minister named Barry H. Downing has sought to prove his theory that the angels of the Bible were actually visitors from other worlds sent to earth to observe mankind and help guide him along his evolutionary path.

Downing, pastor of Northminster Presbyterian Church in Endwell, New York, theorizes that UFO-borne "higher beings" or "angels" are likely from another dimension rather than from other planets, and figured prominently in biblical events ranging from guiding the Israelites out of Egypt to Christ's ascension. The mild-mannered theologian maintains that instead of detracting from the Gospel, acceptance of his theory would do much to strengthen faith and renew confidence in biblical accounts.

"It would establish scientific plausibility for the whole biblical field," Downing explained. "It would reinforce faith and make it possible in a scientific context."

Downing, who holds a doctorate in science and religion from the University of Edinburgh, Scotland, blames the government of the United States for much of the skepticism and mystery surrounding UFOs today. Had the Air Force not prematurely closed its investigation into the UFO phenomenon in 1969, the public would be better informed about the extent of UFO activity, he said.

"If the government weren't lying in denying UFOs exist, we'd have had a religious revolution starting forty years ago," Downing said.

In his book, *The Bible and Flying Saucers,* Downing out-
lines his ideas about God, angels, UFOs, and a coexisting
universe which he believes might be the heavenly hereafter
spoken about so often in the Bible.

"What is clear through the biblical material is that God's
will for the Jews, and eventually for all mankind, was
'revealed' by beings from another world," he wrote. "Usually these beings looked very much like ordinary human
beings (they almost never have wings).... Once the 'package'
of biblical religion had been delivered, man became respon-
sible for the distribution of the contents."

When the Bible was written, Downing observed,
mankind lived in a primitive age, an age in which UFO
phenomena could have easily been misinterpreted as
religious events. For example, he said a group of flying
saucers hovering in a cloudlike formation could have been
seen as the "glowing pillar of fire" that guided the Israelites
out of Egypt. He believes some kind of ray or projecting force
was used to part the Red Sea, enabling the fleeing Israelites
to escape the pharaoh's pursuing army.

"You have to have a good humor about all this," he said.
"I can't prove I'm right, but there's lots of evidence for it, and
until it winds out, some people are just going to have to
laugh."

According to Downing, other UFO-related experiences
recorded in the Bible include the following:

- Prophet Elijah's ascent into heaven aboard a
  "fiery chariot;"
- Ezekiel's vision, in which the writer describes
  a descending spaceship;
- Moses' experience on Mount Sinai in which a
  firelike phenomenon imparted to him the Ten
  Commandments;
- the Star of Bethlehem;
- the engulfing light of Jesus' transfiguration
  and his dramatic ascension into the heavens;
- Paul's blinding vision on the road to Damas-
  cus.

"All these were UFO types of reports," Downing said.

He said postulating such activities in forming biblical faith would open a middle ground between fundamentalist literalism and liberal theory's "demythologizing" of super-natural events as only symbolic.

"It would cut down the distance between liberals and fundamentalists, and serve as a mediating force between the two extremes," he pointed out. "The mythological concepts would have to be reexamined, which would be important for the liberal wing. The conservative wing, which stresses certainty and wants everything locked up tight, also would be impacted. This would mean unlocking things."

Downing, pastor of Northminster Presbyterian Church for more than two decades, also serves as theological consultant to the Mutual UFO network based in Seguin, Texas, and to the Fund for UFO Research, headquartered in Washington. He holds a B.A. in physics and after completing studies at Princeton Theological Seminary he went on to receive his doctorate in Scotland.

When not in the pulpit, Downing spends much of his time writing and lecturing about UFO phenomena. He is particularly critical of the government's decision to shut down Project Blue Book due to "insufficient evidence." He accused the government of "covering up" the results of the investigation, saying the full report was never released to the public.

To support his position, he quotes a letter written by Senator Barry Goldwater in 1975, which states that the material was being withheld as "above Top Secret."

Unlike writers such as Erich von Daniken who, in recent years, have dismissed biblical miracles as the work of star-men from other worlds, Downing clings to his belief that extraterrestrial connections with religious events around the world should only boost faith in the Word of God.

"We could approach religion from a scientific point of view that (in the long run) would unify the church and reinforce faith," he said.

Bizarre Theories

North America: Cradle of Humanity?

ANTHROPOLOGISTS GENERALLY AGREE that mankind originated in Africa at some remote time in the past, and, after millions of years of evolution, eventually migrated to the New World across a now-submerged Asian land bridge about twenty-five thousand years ago.

But hold on.

If that theory is true, what on earth are human footprints doing buried on a Kentucky farm in sediment laid down at least 250 million years ago?

How can it be that workers digging along the Mississippi River once uncovered a slab of sandstone containing a pair of fossilized "humanoid" tracks supposedly millions of years old?

Clearly, if these ancient footprints in stone are genuine, something must be wrong with our fossil record. Otherwise, how is it possible that manlike creatures roamed North America millions of years before the emergence of *Australopithecus* in Africa?

These are only some of the troubling questions being raised in light of several new and not-so-new findings in paleontology, the branch of geology that deals with prehistoric plant and animal fossils. What is slowly emerging is not only the startling possibility that mankind has flourished in the New World for millions of years, but also the astounding proposition that he perhaps walked North America during the time of the dinosaurs.

One of the most compelling pieces of evidence attesting to man's antiquity in the New World was found in a dry river bed near Glen Rose, Texas, shortly after the turn of the century. Residents happened to notice that each time the Paluxy River dried up, giant, manlike footprints, some measuring as much as eighteen inches long and seven inches wide, would show up adjacent to those of dinosaur tracks— irrefutable proof, some said, that forerunners of man had lived during the age of the great reptiles.

In one of the more striking discoveries, the footprints of a manlike creature actually overlapped those of a three-toed dinosaur—a creature that paleontologists insist became extinct more than sixty-six million years ago.

Quick to cash in on the quirky find, some locals began digging up tracks and hawking them to tourists. It is hardly surprising that large numbers of these "tracks" were fakes sold along with authentic tracks to gullible customers. However, many who profited from the business testified their tracks were authentic.

Jim Ryals was one such man. In sworn testimony, Ryals admitted that he and his wife sold fake tracks to tourists, but that some were the real thing. Ryals reportedly told investigators that he and his wife had removed several of the prehistoric human tracks from the Paluxy riverbed, using a chisel and a sledgehammer.

According to Ryals, there was a way that real prints could be distinguished from fakes:

"First, the pressure of the foot usually pushed up a ridge of mud around the outside of the track. Second, if the track is broken open or sawed, pressure lines can be found beneath the surface. Furthermore ... when the (real) tracks were chiseled out of the riverbed, the workman was usually very careful to do his chiseling a good distance from the track, for fear of damaging it. This resulted in a rather wide circle of the limestone surrounding the footprint."

It was common knowledge that local hucksters involved in the lucrative track trade were able to fashion their own versions by carefully copying the authentic models in the riverbed. Some became so skilled at their craft that it became difficult for even trained scientists to tell the real tracks from the phonies.

Understandably, most scientists are reluctant to even consider the authenticity of the Glen Rose tracks, since dinosaurs supposedly died off millions of years before the evolution of *Homo sapiens* from small, warm-blooded creatures called mammals. Others who have looked at the evidence are not so skeptical.

In 1976, Jack Walper, a professor of geology at Texas Christian University, conducted studies that offered additional proof that the human prints were genuine. In a series of tests, he showed that the pressure of each fossilized footfall had forced the mud upward—indicating that actual human beings had made the prints at some time in the past contemporary with dinosaurs.

But the truth behind the Glen Rose tracks remains a mystery, as do some other startling finds linking man to a very ancient past in North America. Shortly before the outbreak of World War II, for example, Dr. Wilbur Burroughs, head of the geology department of Berea College in Kentucky, discovered what he called "humanoid" footprints in carboniferous sandstone on a farm belonging to O. Finnel in the hills of Rockcastle County, Kentucky.

Special tests on the Rockcastle tracks revealed no signs of carving or artificial marking in or around the prints, suggesting that the prints were authentic. The prints—found in rock estimated to be more than 250 million years old—were later destroyed by vandals.

During the War of 1812, noted American ethnologist Henry R. Schoolcraft excavated a pair of human footprints from a quarry along the Mississippi River near St. Louis. Schoolcraft, who found the tracks in a limestone deposit estimated to be 270 million years old, described them as "strikingly natural, exhibiting every muscular impression, and swell of the heel and toes, with a precision and faithfulness to nature, which I have not been able to copy, with perfect exactness."

For years, some anthropologists have argued that the traditionally accepted time frame of man's arrival in the New World simply does not fit the facts and is no longer valid. Jeffrey Goodman, an engineering archaeologist from Tucson, Arizona, believes he has found evidence to prove that man first developed in North America, then migrated westward toward Asia and the Old World.

Goodman bases his theory on many individual bits and pieces of information in the archaeological record which, taken together, serve to fingerprint and document specific migrations in reverse.

"Based on the evidence now coming to light, I believe that there was migration in reverse. Instead of nomadic hunters coming from the Old World to populate the New World, the first fully modern men anywhere in the world traveled to the Old World and woke it from its sound, evolutionary sleep."

Not even Goodman, however, nor any of the other "America First" theorists can adequately account for the enigmatic presence of human footprints in stone deposits believed to be many millions of years old. These timeless tracks in stone remain one of the mysteries of our age.

The Flat Earth

CENTURIES AGO, MANY PEOPLE believed that if a ship sailed too far from shore, it would fall off the edge of the earth. This was due to the belief, accepted by the majority of European scholars in post-classical times, that the earth was flat.

Few people argued with the concept. After all, weren't the "four corners of the earth" mentioned in the Bible?

And wasn't it true that few mariners ever reached the terrible edge of the earth because of what stood in the way—hungry sea serpents, monstrous whirlpools, and boiling lakes of fire?

These and other beliefs kept ancient man close to shore until 1492, when Christopher Columbus made his famous voyage.

As far as we know, the admiral encountered no sea serpents, dangerous whirlpools, or boiling lakes of fire. Neither did he sail off the edge of the earth—thus proving, once and for all, that the earth was round, not flat.

Still, the flat earth theory did not entirely fade away with Columbus's epic discovery or those of subsequent navigators, including Ferdinand Magellan, whose ships were the first to circumnavigate the globe in the 1500s.

Throughout the seventeenth, eighteenth, and nineteenth centuries, various groups of people, some of them deadly serious, continued to deny the existence of a spherical world. They scoffed at the great voyages, claiming that most of them were either elaborate hoaxes or out-and-out lies.

To think otherwise, they reasoned, would be contrary to common sense and, more importantly, to God's teachings.

Even today, when satellites orbit the earth and fast-going ocean liners and supersonic aircraft whiz back and forth around the globe, there are those who still insist the earth is flat. Some of these people—known as flatearthers—say science has yet to prove otherwise.

In the 1940s, one particular group of flatearthers attracted international attention because of its offer to pay five thousand dollars to anyone who proved the earth was round. Led by a charismatic, almost fanatical preacher named Wilbur Glenn Voliva, the group settled in Zion, Illinois, a few miles north of Chicago, and founded a church to promote its unorthodox doctrine.

Rabidly fundamentalist, Voliva ruled Zion with an iron hand. Under his guidance, the town was soon governed by a notorious set of blue laws that would have made the Salem Puritans proud.

For example, anyone caught smoking or wearing shorts on the streets could go to jail. Alcohol was banned, as were gambling, swearing, and whistling in public on Sunday. Zion speed traps became legendary throughout the area.

As the town's virtual dictator, Voliva proclaimed his own special belief that the earth was shaped like a pancake, with the North Pole in the center and the South Pole distributed around the circumference.

A solid wall of ice kept ships from falling off the edge of the earth, he explained.

To spread his word to the faithful, Voliva published books, magazines, and newspaper articles outlining in detail his complex theories.

The self-styled preacher, who denounced other fundamentalists as "liars," also believed that the stars were small, flat bodies and not very far away. The moon, he said, was lighted from within. He dismissed the notion of the sun's great distance from earth by saying, "The idea of a sun millions of miles in diameter and ninety-one million miles away is silly."

On the contrary, he said, the sun was only thirty-two miles across and not more than three thousand miles from earth.

"It stands to reason it must be so," he noted. "God made the sun to light the earth, and therefore must have placed it close to the task it was designed to do. What would you think of a man who built a house in Zion and put the lamp to light it in Kenosha, Wisconsin?"

Voliva believed in a small, comfortable universe, one that was familiar and "made common sense." In a 1930 magazine published by Voliva's church, the Christian Apostolic Church of Zion, there is a photograph of Lake Winnebago, Wisconsin. The caption reads: "Anyone can go to Oshkosh and see the sight for themselves any clear day.

"With a good pair of binoculars," the caption continues, "one can see small objects on the opposite shore, proving beyond any doubt that the surface of the lake is a plane, or a horizontal line.... The scientific value of this picture is enormous."

Even though Voliva traveled frequently, often taking trips around the world himself, he never accepted the concept of a spherical planet. In fact, he eagerly offered to pay "handsome money" to anyone who could prove the world was round. He never paid a cent.

By the 1930s, the volcanic minister's hold on his flock had begun to slip. His infamous "blue laws" had infuriated so many church members as well as outsiders that a campaign was launched to force him to step down from the pulpit.

Annoyed but never remorseful, Voliva retired. At a final gathering of the faithful, he told them that he planned to live to the ripe old age of 120 years. God would take care of him, he noted, because of a special dietary regimen he had adhered to all his life.

He died in 1942 at the age of seventy-two.

Do Stones Hold Clue to Fate of Eleanor Dare?

MUCH HAS BEEN WRITTEN and said about the lost colony of Roanoke, Sir Walter Raleigh's ill-fated attempt to settle Virginia in the late sixteenth century.

To this day, however, no one really knows what happened to the band of brave men, women, and children who settled along the lonely shores of the New World wilderness. Their disappearance remains one of America's greatest unsolved historical mysteries.

In Raleigh's time, "Virginia" referred to much of the land lying north of Spanish-controlled Florida. Named after Elizabeth I—the "Virgin Queen"—the colony was set up to serve as a base while Elizabethan explorers sought gold and a fabled passageway to the Orient.

Instead of gold and a linkup with the Pacific, the Roanoke Islanders found hardship and suffering. Had it not been for friendly Indians, the effort might have failed even sooner.

In 1587 John White, the governor of the colony, sailed away to England for fresh supplies. As fate would have it, war broke out with Spain and he was unable to return until three years later.

Imagine the governor's profound surprise when finally he landed at Roanoke only to find the New World outpost abandoned and in ruins! The only clue to the colonists' whereabouts was the word "Croatoan" carved into a tree—

an indication, perhaps, that the colonists had fled to the Indians on a nearby island when supplies ran low.

But the Croatoans expressed no knowledge of the colonists, nor did any other regional tribe questioned. They had simply disappeared—vanished without a trace from the historical record.

In the 1930s, the president of Brenau College in Georgia stepped forward with a shocking new theory. Using as evidence a freshly excavated stone, Dr. Haywood Pearce, Jr. postulated that some of the colonists had migrated to Georgia.

Engraved on the twenty-pound stone in his possession were Elizabethan markings, including the initials of Eleanor White Dare—Governor White's daughter, who had been among the missing colonists. When news of Pearce's discovery leaked out, other stones with Eleanor's initials on them began turning up in Georgia and elsewhere—forty-nine in all.

Sensationalized newspaper and magazine stories about "Eleanor Dare's diary" appeared as more and more stones surfaced.

According to Pearce, the stones were subjected to "every scientific test I could command" to verify their authenticity. Stonecutters concurred that the inscriptions could not have been duplicated with modern techniques. Geologists matched the age of the work with that of Governor White's time. Specialists in Elizabethan English were called in to confirm the authenticity of the script.

Finally, a panel of distinguished historians led by Dr. Samuel Eliot Morison spent months studying the stones, finally concluding that "the preponderance of evidence points to the authenticity of the stones."

Following Morison's announcement, dozens of other stones surfaced in several different states. The discoveries generated so much nationwide publicity that some scholars started seriously questioning their validity.

The stones finally came under fire in 1940 when the Saturday Evening Post commissioned a reporter to investigate the story. Journalist Boyden Sparkes uncovered evidence suggesting that Pearce, Morison, and other investigators had been duped into believing the stones were authentic.

For one thing, the geologist who tested the stones later admitted to Sparkes that markings on at least one of them had been carved quite recently. The authority on Elizabethan English then told Sparkes that some of the words found on the stones "probably" had not been introduced into the English language until centuries later.

According to Sparkes, at least one stonecutter acknowledged that such work could have been faked quite easily.

The final blow came when it was revealed that one of the first men to find a stone had been accused of faking copies and trying to sell them to museums. The same man had apparently engraved antique-looking inscriptions on stones, planting several of them in the area as a publicity stunt.

The "mystery" of the Eleanore Dare stones had been solved.

Not so, however, the true fate of the governor's daughter, her husband, her child, and the hundred or so other doomed colonists of Roanoke Island.

The Father of Atlantology

SINCE ANCIENT TIMES, men have dreamed of lost cities and vanished civilizations, of glittering kingdoms beyond the horizon where forgotten secrets and fabulous treasures were there for the taking.

But for all the allure of these fabled lands, however, none rivals the spell cast by Atlantis, the legendary island in the Atlantic which, according to the Greek philosopher, Plato, sank beneath the waves during a cataclysmic upheaval some ten thousand years ago.

And of all the champions of the Atlantis story, none defended it more vigorously or passionately than a failed-businessman-turned-politician from Philadelphia named Ignatius Loyola Donnelly.

In 1882, more than twenty-three hundred years after Plato first wrote about Atlantis, Donnelly published a book in which he set out to prove not only the existence of Atlantis, but also his theory that the Atlanteans were the first men to achieve civilization and that the deities of various ancient mythologies were in fact the actual royalty of the doomed continent.

The book, *Atlantis: the Antediluvian World,* was an instant international bestseller. In spite of its scholarly shortcomings, sales continued to soar year after year, eliciting acclaim from the likes of William Gladstone, the British prime minister. By 1890, the United States market had gobbled up twenty-three editions, and twenty-six had appeared in England.

To Donnelly, Atlantis was the world that preceded the Biblical Flood. Situated somewhere far beyond the Pillars of Hercules (two headlands on either side of the Straits of Gibraltar) the Atlantean kingdom had been the Garden of Eden, the Elysian Fields, the home of powerful kings and queens who were later to become the gods of the Egyptians, the Greeks, the Phoenicians, the Hindus, the Scandinavians, and the American Indians.

The people of Atlantis, Donnelly wrote, were handsome, prosperous, technologically advanced sun-worshippers. Their oldest colony was probably Egypt, whose civilization reproduced that of the mother kingdom. The Atlantean alphabet inspired that of the Phoenicians, believed by many to be the parent of all European alphabets.

But all was not well on Atlantis, Donnelly pointed out. Society deteriorated while corrupt politicians led the population down the road to depravity and decadence. One day approximately ten thousand years ago, the entire island—along with most of its inhabitants—was destroyed by a series of earthquakes and tidal waves.

When Atlantis perished "in that terrible convulsion of nature," a few citizens escaped in ships and on rafts, bearing the dreadful news to the nations of both east and west; hence, the stories of the Great Flood which are told all over the world.

As Donnelly saw it, these Atlantean refugees planted the seeds for the creation of many new civilizations—in Egypt, in India, in Central America, and elsewhere.

Although his controversial book catapulted him to fame and fortune, life had not always been so kind to the dreamy Philadelphian. Until he withdrew from politics to write about Atlantis, Donnelly's life had been one long roller coaster ride.

Born in 1831 to impoverished Irish immigrants, Donnelly became a lawyer and entered politics in his early twenties. In 1856 he moved to Minnesota, where he and a friend tried unsuccessfully to develop a metropolis grandly dubbed Nininger City. The city failed, so once again the short, red-haired orator turned to politics, first as lieutenant governor and then, three years later, as a United States congressman.

In the late 1870s, Donnelly ran afoul due to post-Civil War political turmoil and dropped out of politics altogether. On his forty-ninth birthday, broke, dispirited, his political ambitions in tatters, Donnelly sat down and wrote, "All my hopes are gone, and the future settles down upon me dark and gloomy indeed."

Little did he realize at the time that his future was about to take off in a different direction.

As a congressman in Washington, Donnelly had spent countless hours in the Library of Congress, pouring over the latest books and scientific journals dealing with geology, history, folklore, world literature, religion, and linguistics. It was there that the idea for a book about Atlantis began to take shape.

Specifically, he was drawn to the many similarities between the Old and New Worlds—botanical, biological, and cultural. Why, he wondered, did so many American and European animals and plants look alike? Why the coincidence of pyramids, pillars, burial mounds, and ships appearing on both sides of the Atlantic?

Donnelly's answer was that everything had originated on Atlantis. "I cannot believe," he wrote, "that the great inventions were duplicated spontaneously ... in different countries. If this were so, all savages would have invented the boomerang; all savages would possess pottery, bows and arrows, slings, tents and canoes; in short, all races would have risen to civilization, for certainly the comforts of life are as agreeable to one people as another."

As popular as Donnelly's vision of the lost continent was on both sides of the Atlantic, he knew that his research was incomplete. What he needed was tangible evidence.

"A single engraved tablet dredged up from Plato's island would be worth more to science, would more strike the imagination of mankind, than all the gold of Peru, all the monuments of Egypt, and all the terra-cotta fragments gathered from the great libraries of Chaldea," he wrote.

Encouraged by the favorable reception of his book and lectures, Donnelly reentered politics and twice ran for the vice-presidency of the United States on the ticket of the Populist Party he helped to found. Although his political success was at a dead end, he had laid the groundwork for his successors in a new, esoteric field of study: Atlantology.

The Bottomless Depths

IN HIS NOVEL, *Journey to the Center of the Earth,* author Jules Verne described an imaginary world far below the earth's surface, a kind of "netherworld," filled with prehistoric beasts, gushing underground streams, and quivering rock formations that sometimes collapsed and sank unexpectedly beneath one's feet.

Like many other people, Verne was fascinated by these strange subterranean realms and by the possibility that life might exist in the uncharted depths below. His fictional accounts of underground life forms and landscapes helped spark interest in the study of caves and especially in the peculiar natural phenomena known as sinkholes.

Sinkholes exist in nearly every part of the world. They are especially common in the southeastern United States, where limestone deposits exist in great numbers and new ones are constantly forming. In Alabama, for example, at least four thousand sinkholes have been formed since 1900.

The sudden appearance of sinkholes can—and often does—result in horrifying consequences. Trees, automobiles, buildings, and even swimming pools have been known to vanish within these gaping cavities that occasionally develop and consume with frightening speed.

One of the most disastrous sinkholes on record occurred in Winter Park, Florida, in the summer of 1981. Mae Rose Owens, who was feeding her dog in the back yard, was the first person to notice that something strange was going on in her neighborhood.

"I saw a tree—a very large tree—just fall into a hole and disappear from sight," the woman said.

Mrs. Owens watched in horror while other trees and shrubbery plunged into the newly formed hole. The hole grew and grew, she said, until it eventually swallowed her home, part of an auto repair shop, five Porsche automobiles parked on its lot, a pickup truck, the deep end of an Olympic-size municipal swimming pool, and a stand of trees.

The woman said she hated to imagine what would have happened had people not noticed the hole forming and scampered out of the way in time.

When the hole finally stopped growing about twenty-four hours later, it measured 350 feet wide and 125 feet deep. More than 160 thousand cubic yards of earth had been devoured—enough to fill sixty-four hundred dump trucks! Damage was estimated in excess of two million dollars.

Fortunately, disasters like that which occurred in Winter Park are rare. But scientists say the potential for repeat performances is very great, especially in areas where large quantities of underground water have slowly seeped into limestone bedrock.

The problem starts when the water-saturated limestone develops cavities. Surface soil weighing down on the weakened limestone eventually caves it in, taking with it whatever else is on top—cars, buildings, trees, animals, or people.

Low-lying Florida, which already has thousands of small sinkholes dotting its landscape, is particularly vulnerable to future formations. One-third of the Sunshine State is riddled by eroded limestone, most of it lying at a shallow depth and thus subject to the collapse of surface soil at any time.

But Florida is not alone. At least fifteen other states, including Pennsylvania, Louisiana, Mississippi, Georgia, Alabama, and Kentucky, have similar problems. In Kentucky, sinkholes have created a vast area of unstable terrain, and scientists there say it is a disaster waiting to happen.

Tens of thousands of similar sinkholes honeycomb the Caribbean islands, some of which have created basins many miles across and pits more than a thousand feet deep. Other large sinkholes exist in China, South Africa, Greece, South America, and elsewhere.

In the past, sinkholes were regarded as mysterious places where supernatural powers were at work. Some people believed they were doorways to a netherworld populated by demons, giants, and dragons.

Most American Indians who knew about sinkholes avoided them. Some, however, constructed elaborate religious rituals around them, occasionally offering human sacrifices.

Over the years, scientists have learned a lot about these phenomena. They know, for example, that sinkholes are caused by drainage of underground water, and they also know how to identify areas susceptible to the problem.

What they don't know, however, is how to predict when a sinkhole will occur and how to prevent a sudden, disastrous collapse. This lack of knowledge could prove costly should a sudden collapse strike an inhabited area or a major structure such as an airport or large dam.

Scientists armed with radar, seismic detectors, acoustic resonance sensors, and a variety of other geologic sensing devices are working overtime to ward off such a science fiction scenario. In spite of high-tech equipment, however, some doomsayers predict it is only a matter of time before a disaster of awesome proportions strikes.

The finger is usually pointed at overdeveloped, fragile regions such as Florida.

And with fifteen percent of the earth's surface resting on terrain susceptible to sinkholes, who knows?

History's Mysteries

The Black Spot

THE ROAD TOWARD civil war between North and South was long and painful, with good men on both sides sincerely convinced of the rightness of their cause.

One such man was John C. Calhoun, the ex-vice-president and fiery senator from South Carolina whose impassioned stand on states' rights, slavery, and nullification earned him a reputation as the South's leading intellectual architect of secession.

Although he went to his grave a decade before the guns sounded at Fort Sumter in the spring of 1861, Calhoun apparently had a premonition of the coming conflict.

The chilling forewarning had apparently come to the aging senator in a dream shortly before his death in 1850. Details of the dream were recounted over breakfast one morning to his long-time friend, fellow fire-eater and states' right advocate Robert Toombs of Georgia.

Toombs knew something was wrong the moment he sat down next to Calhoun. For one thing, he had never seen the old War Hawk so worn and pale. It was obvious, the Georgian later noted, that something was bothering his old friend, for not only did he look as if he hadn't slept in days, he also kept tugging at his right hand for no apparent reason.

Concerned, the Georgia senator asked if anything was wrong.

"Pshaw!" Calhoun retorted, almost as if he were embarrassed by his strange affliction. "It is nothing but a dream I had last night which makes me see now a large black spot, like an ink blotch, upon the back of my right hand."

Calhoun, who then carefully concealed the troubled hand, called it "an optical illusion, I suppose."

Toombs responded, "What was your dream like? I am not very superstitious about dreams, but sometimes they have a great deal of truth in them."

Calhoun leaned back in his chair and sighed. He then began to unravel one of the strangest tales Toombs had ever heard.

"At a late hour last night," Calhoun said, "as I was sitting in my room writing, I was astonished by the entrance of a visitor, who, without a word, took a seat opposite me. The manner in which the intruder entered, so perfectly self-possessed, as though my room and all within it belonged to him, excited in me as much surprise as indignation."

Calhoun said that he had watched as the intruder drew closer. Then he made a startling discovery.

"As I raised my head to look into his features, I discovered that he was wrapped in a thin cloak which effectively concealed his face."

In a soft, peculiar tone the stranger asked, "What are you writing, senator from South Carolina?"

Calhoun replied that he was "writing a plan for the dissolution of the American Union."

"Senator from South Carolina," the presence whispered in a voice that crackled like the wind, "will you allow me to look at your right hand?"

At that moment the figure rose and his cloak fell away.

Calhoun slumped backward, terrified by what he saw.

"I saw his face. The sight struck me like a thunderclap. It was the face of a dead man whom extraordinary events had called back to life. The features were those of George Washington and he was dressed in a general's uniform."

As if in a dream, Calhoun extended his right hand, as requested. He said a "strange thrill" passed through his body as the specter grasped his hand and held it to the light.

"After holding my hand for a moment, he looked at me steadily and said in a quiet way, 'And with this right hand, senator from South Carolina, you would sign your name to a paper declaring the Union dissolved?'"

"Yes," Calhoun replied, "if a certain contingency arises."

At that moment a mysterious black blotch appeared on the back of his hand.

Alarmed, the senator asked, "What is that?"

"That," the stranger replied, "is the mark by which Benedict Arnold is known in the next world."

Suddenly the cloaked stranger disappeared, and Calhoun awoke in his bed. He sat up and glanced around the room. It was empty. The ghostly intruder was gone.

Then, recalling the dream, he slowly turned his eyes to the back of his right hand. What he saw made him gasp.

The black spot was still there—just as it had been during the dream!

The Strange Case of Major Lynch

FOR MORE THAN TWO centuries, the ancient hills of Franklin County, North Carolina, have shielded a dark and terrible secret from the outside world.

It was here, according to legend, that the first overt act in America was committed against British rule, almost a decade before the Boston Tea Party and six years before the misnamed Boston Massacre.

It was also here that a daring but reckless young English army officer named Lynch came face to face with his worst nightmare—an angry mob of backwoods patriots with fire in their eyes and a noose in their hands. The grisly fate that befell the young officer would become the stuff of legend, whispered about in the dark of night around lonely campfires and crackling hearths.

The tragic ordeal of Major Lynch, whose first name escapes history, reads like a classic tale of mystery involving kidnapping, a torchlight trial, murder, and a coverup.

In fact, the details of the case were covered up so well that even today the unfortunate demise of Major Lynch is the subject of much debate among scholars and authorities on folklore.

Two questions arise: did a Major Lynch actually exist, and if so, was he actually hanged—or "lynched," as that method of mob execution would come to be called in his "honor"?

It seems certain that there was a young officer fitting Lynch's description, a tax collector by trade, sent to this remote region by the royal governor to seize property from colonials behind on their tax payments.

In those days, more than a decade before the events at Lexington and Concord, Americans did not take kindly to any of the king's efforts to raise revenue among the hard pressed colonies. So, understandably, it was a less than enthusiastic crowd that turned out on a cold, snowy day in 1764 to greet the dashing and somewhat daring major upon his arrival. From behind closed doors and shutters, people watched and waited for the officer's first move.

They did not have to wait long. Only days after his arrival, the brash young officer quickly confiscated stores of tobacco, corn, and other commodities owned by a local farmer who happened to be delinquent in his taxes.

The locals were outraged, so outraged they started plotting revenge. Something surely had to be done, they reasoned, or their own property might be next. Where would it all end?

Furthermore, who gave this man, an Englishman, the right to seize an American's property in the first place?

The answer to that question, of course, was the old king himself, George III. In an effort to rectify England's financial problems left over from the Seven Years' War, the temperamental monarch put together a series of sweeping revenue-raising measures designed to force the Americans to pick up part of the tab for stationing British troops on American soil.

As far as the Americans were concerned, this was "taxation without representation." From Boston to Savannah, radical patriots vowed to resist paying any new taxes.

But while other patriots at this stage only talked about it, the good citizens of Bute County—as Franklin County was called before its name was changed after the war—took swift action.

In twos and threes they started quietly gathering on street corners to discuss the situation. Dozens gathered at churches, in the local tavern, and on front porches. Rumors circulated that the hated English agent was planning to seize additional property.

Late that afternoon, armed with guns and swords, they set off toward the tax agent's office. Beneath a cold, snowy sky they marched, torchlights blazing, fists clenched.

One grim-faced colonial carried a thick rope.

When word reached the major that the group of armed and angry colonials were heading his way, his first impulse was to stand and confront the mob. But after some consideration, he wisely decided to flee; he had heard too many tales about how dangerous these backwoods ruffians could be when cornered.

Out of the back door of his office he ran, to where the horses were tied. Panic-stricken, the major realized there wasn't even time to hitch up a mount, so he took off on foot into the dark woods as fast as his two legs could carry him.

A few hours later, so the story goes, the pursuing rebels found him hiding under a bridge spanning Red Bug Creek, about fourteen miles from where the county seat of Louisburg now stands. The colonials bound and gagged the tax agent and hauled him off to the home of one Benjamin Perry to stand trial before a committee of citizens.

The trial lasted only a few minutes. Lynch was found guilty of unspecified crimes, then marched two miles to a point north of Louisburg and hanged on an oak tree near the spot where a creek enters into the Tar River.

It is reasonable to assume that the unlawful hanging of the English officer named Lynch resulted in a new term in the English language—"lynch law." According to local tradition, the name of the small creek where the officer was hanged was soon changed to Lynch Creek to commemorate the first act of defiance in America against British rule—and to mark the spot where the first blood was spilled in the revolution.

However interesting this story might be, not all historians are convinced of its accuracy. Some believe the story about Major Lynch is only a "fairy tale," as one researcher put it. Another, John H. Wheeler, author of *Memoirs of*

Eminent North Carolinians, noted that a famous Tory named Beard was hanged on Lynch Creek during the Revolutionary War by command of Benjamin Seawell.

It is Wheeler's contention that the term "lynch law" originated from this event.

However, research indicates that Beard's untimely end along the lonely banks of Lynch Creek came at least a decade after Major Lynch's legendary hanging—proof enough, argue some, that the name originated with Major Lynch's own death and no other.

But if the grisly story is true, then why was it kept a secret from the outside world for so long? Some authorities suggest that colonials, fearful of reprisals from royal authorities, deliberately kept a lid on the murder.

Although the facts soon became obscure, the story of Major Lynch and his untimely demise remains one of this region's most intriguing and enduring legends.

The Most Mysterious Manuscript in the World

IN 1912, A NEW YORK DEALER in rare books by the name of Wilfrid M. Voynich was vacationing in Italy when word reached him about a mysterious old volume said to be in the possession of a nearby college library.

According to Voynich's sources, the book was extemely old and filled with strange drawings and writings and formulas that no man living or dead had been able to decipher. Rumor had it that the book had once belonged to Roger Bacon, the medieval philosopher and alchemist known respectfully as "Doctor Mirabilis," who reportedly had discovered how to turn base metal into gold.

One expert even suggested that the enigmatic script and illustrations contained in the old book explained Bacon's long-lost formula!

Since old books were his business, Voynich, a slight, bespectacled man in his mid-forties, decided he must see the book for himself and, if possible, buy it. If he could somehow authenticate the publication date and ownership, the book might be worth a fortune back in the states.

At the Mondragone College Library he befriended a librarian who agreed to show him the book. The moment he laid eyes on the frail volume gathering dust on a shelf in a back room, Voynich knew he was onto something special—perhaps even priceless.

The librarian told him that no one knew who had written it, when it had been published, or even the language in which it was written.

Quivering with excitement, the American book dealer couldn't believe his good fortune as he gently thumbed through the quaint volume, struck not only by its age and quality of design, but also by the unusual drawings and mysterious, flowing text that filled its pages. It was written in a language neither Voynich nor any of his linguistic associates had ever seen before.

Voynich concluded that the manuscript, measuring five by eight inches and consisting of about two hundred pages, must be written in some kind of code. Its quaint, vellum leaves were covered with an extraordinary style of writing— extraordinary because the author had used a completely unknown alphabet!

Each graceful line of text, highlighted by stylized swirls and enigmatic adornments, fairly flowed across the page, broken up at odd places by beautifully rendered black-and-white illustrations. Since most of the drawings represented plants, astronomical configurations, and female anatomy, it was assumed that the manuscript might have been some sort of treatise on the medicinal or curative powers of plants.

Deeply intrigued, Voynich purchased the book and took it back to New York. There he invited a number of friends and literary scholars to examine its pages. Chemists, historians, and more linguists spent hours pouring over the puzzling tome, trying to determine not only the message of the book, but also its age and author.

Alas, the harder they tried to unravel the secrets of the little volume, the less they knew.

Fortunately, an old letter had been included in the sale of the book to Voynich. Supposedly written in 1666, the letter purported to be from Marcus Marci, rector of the University of Prague, to Athanasius Kircher. Since both men were leading scientists of their day, the letter—and book—were believed to contain something of great value.

In the letter, Marci wrote that he had obtained the manuscript from "an intimate friend" and was sending it to Kircher, his former tutor, "for I was convinced it could be read by no one except yourself."

To add to the mystery, Marci said the book had once been owned by the Holy Roman Emperor Rudolf II, who died in 1612. Rudolf allegedly paid a large sum of money for the book, which he believed to have been written by Roger Bacon, the English scientist and writer who had lived in the thirteenth century.

Bacon was reportedly centuries ahead of his time and has been given credit for having predicted many features of twentieth-century life, including automobiles and airplanes. Bacon was also a renowned philosopher and alchemist. Could Voynich's mysterious manuscript be one of Bacon's unknown works—a scientific treatise, perhaps, containing novel theories too radical and advanced for his own time— such as the secret of transforming base metal into gold?

In the 1970s, Robert S. Brumbaugh at Yale University noticed that some of the symbols of the Voynich Manuscript appeared to follow a numeric sequence. Looking closer, Brumbaugh then found some doodled calculations in the margins of the manuscript, including a chart with twenty-six symbols—the number of letters in the alphabet.

By cross-indexing the symbols in the chart with those in the doodles, Brumbaugh came to the conclusion that they were a perfect match. Much of the language in the book turned out to be a kind of simplified Latin with the words frequently ending in the suffix -*us*.

Today the book is in the possession of the Beinecke Rare Book and Manuscript Library at Yale University. Hardly a day goes by without at least one inquiry about the Voynich Manuscript, regarded by many as the most mysterious manuscript in the world.

The Lost Treasure of the Confederacy

ON A QUIET SUNDAY morning in the spring of 1865, a messenger entered St. Paul's Church in Richmond, Virginia, and placed a telegram in the hands of a distinguished gentleman seated in the front row.

After reading the message the gentleman picked up his hat and quickly left. He headed straight for the executive offices of the Confederate government, where he hurriedly assembled the secretary of the treasury and other top-level officers for a secret meeting.

The man was Jefferson Davis, president of the Confederate States of America. The fateful message he had received was from General Robert E. Lee, informing the president that Richmond was in danger of falling into the hands of Federal forces.

Lee's advice was that Davis evacuate the Confederate capital city as soon as possible.

Davis agreed and hastily issued three orders: his family was to be whisked away to safety; all executive papers were to be either destroyed or removed; and finally, immediate steps were to be taken to safeguard funds in the Confederate treasury.

The president's last order—the disposal of the treasury—was destined to become one of the most controversial issues in Confederate history. So much has been speculated and written about the fate of the funds that the story has become ingrained in Southern folklore and myth.

No one really knows what happened to the uncounted millions in gold, silver, and cash left over from efforts to finance the doomed Confederate government.

To this day, scholars continue to debate not only the whereabouts of the missing treasure, but also its exact amount. It is well known that the bulk of the loot—estimated by some sources at 2.5 million dollars—apparently followed Davis on his retreat southward through the Carolinas and Georgia, making stops at Danville, Virginia; Greensboro, North Carolina; Charlotte, North Carolina; Chester, Newberry and Abbeville, South Carolina; Augusta, Georgia; and finally at Washington, Georgia, where the last meeting of the Confederate cabinet was held.

For years after the war, stories persisted that Davis himself appropriated the funds for his private use. That theory received top billing when one of his former generals, Joseph E. Johnston, suggested to a newspaper reporter that much of the money had been stolen by Davis and other high-ranking Confederate officials.

Even though Johnston's words seriously undermined the ex-president's character in the minds of many, few scholars accepted the general's version then—or now—as fact.

Writing in the *Georgia Historical Quarterly* in 1918, author Otis Ashmore disputed Johnston's much-publicized charge, insisting that attempts to link the ill-fated president of the Confederacy with the missing treasure were nonsense.

"Writers and thinkers may differ concerning the wisdom of Mr. Davis' political theories and policies, but of his honor, his courage, and his purity of character there can not be the slightest question," he wrote.

Neither, added Ashmore, was there evidence that any of the missing funds were misappropriated by other Confederate officials.

"These reflections have been completely and satisfactorily answered," he continued. "And no fair minded man in the clear light of the convincing facts can accuse Mr. Davis of misappropriating a single dollar of public funds."

As to what happened to the treasure, speculation continues to abound. But evidence provided by Ashmore and other scholars seems to bear out the assertion that a considerable amount—if not all—was used to pay off war veterans, while the rest was hidden either in England or somewhere west of the Mississippi to be drawn upon upon should the South resume its struggle with the North at a future date.

Some investigators maintain that the bulk of this hidden loot was captured by advancing Union soldiers.

Records exist—many of them signed by Secretary of the Treasury Reagan and other high-ranking cabinet officers and generals—showing that considerable sums of the money were paid out to soldiers to help finance their long journey home from the front lines once the war was over.

By the time the treasure convoy reached Washington, where the final disbursement of funds supposedly took place, the once-impressive fortune had dwindled down to the following amounts, according to Reagan: $85,000 in gold coin and bullion; $35,000 in silver coin; $36,000 in silver bullion; $7,000 in Confederate treasury notes; and $18,000 in pound sterling.

Even if this was all that was left, the question remains: what happened to these funds?

That answer might be summarized in a post-war letter in which Reagan wrote to Davis, "I directed an acting treasurer [in Washington] to turn over to two of our naval officers ... most of the gold coin and bullion; with the understanding between us all before you left Washington, that as soon as the excitement subsided a little, they were to take this out to Bermuda or Liverpool, and turn it over to our agents, that we might draw against it after we should get across the Mississippi river."

Adding to the mystery, however, were comments made by Reagan's successor, M.H. Clark of Clarksville, Tennessee, in an interview with the Louisville *Courier-Journal* dated January 13, 1882. In the interview Clark denied that the Confederate treasury had ever been as flush as originally suggested by Reagan.

"If the treasury at Richmond had contained 2.5 million dollars in coin, certainly the brave men of our armies would never have suffered so severely from want of sufficient food and clothing as they did during the winter of 1864-65, for it had been demonstrated that gold could draw food and raiment from without the lines."

Regardless of the amount, however, and although President Davis's name has been cleared of suspicion by most historians, the "missing" Confederate treasure remains one of the Deep South's greatest unsolved mysteries.

Ancient Artifacts in the New World

ARCHEOLOGISTS ARE FAIRLY certain that various groups of Vikings sailed to the New World centuries before Christopher Columbus made his historic landfall on San Salvador in 1492.

Remains of Viking villages in Canada and elsewhere illustrate the roving habits of these early voyagers who may have sailed as far south as Savannah, Georgia, a thousand years ago before abandoning their colonial aspirations.

But compelling new evidence unearthed in Georgia, Alabama, Pennsylvania, and several other eastern states suggests that the Vikings might have been Johnny-come-latelies on the American scene, that roaming bands of ancient seafarers from the Mediterranean might have preceded them by more than two thousand years.

The evidence begins with a small lead tablet covered with what some scholars believe is Sumerian cuneiform writing. The tablet, discovered near La Grange, Georgia, in 1964, bears a date denoting the year 43 of the reign of Sulgi, a Third Dynasty Sumerian king.

According to Barry Fell, author of *America B.C.* and *Saga America,* that date is equivalent to 2040 B.C.

Three years after the discovery of the La Grange tablet, Manfred L. Metcalf found a strange piece of Chattahoochee Valley sandstone near his home in Columbus, Georgia. The stone, which was dug out of the chimney of a nineteenth-century home, was inscribed with symbols resembling Linear A, a writing system used by the Minoans of Crete.

According to most authorities, the Linear A style of writing went out of use in the Mediterranean about 1500 B.C.

In 1957, a young boy out looking for arrowheads came across an odd-shaped bronze coin along the banks of the Chattahoochee River near Coweta Falls. After the boy traded the artifact for candy, it subsequently came into the possession of a University of Georgia instructor named Preston L. Blackwell.

Blackwell identified the coin as Carthaginian in origin, similar to dozens of others found in Arkansas, Pennsylvania, Alabama, and Connecticut, as well as in Great Britain.

During the centuries they maintained naval control of the western Mediterranean, the Carthaginians prohibited foreign ships from sailing through the Strait of Gilbraltar. According to Dr. Fell, this blockade assured them of a monopoly in a vast trade area.

After defeating Carthage in the Punic Wars (264-146 B.C.), the Romans succeeded in becoming the dominant naval power in the region. Some experts believe Roman naval expeditions sailed far beyond the Pillars of Hercules on the Strait of Gibraltar, eventually reaching lands as far west as America.

According to Dr. Joseph Mahan, author of *The Secret*, a Roman coin found in 1945 by a Columbus, Georgia, woman offers evidence of Roman influence reaching across the Atlantic. Mahan said the coin has been positively identified as belonging to the reign of Antoninus Pius (138-161 A.D.).

"This coin is part of a growing collection of Roman artifacts being found at sites throughout the continental United States," Mahan said.

In another discovery, possibly related to the coin found in Columbus, a cache of Roman ceramic lamps and pottery was unearthed in the 1930s by two young boys in a cavern on the bank of the Coosa River near Gadsden, Alabama.

Predictably, these startling discoveries, as well as others linked to ancient Egyptians, Basques, Phoenicians, Libyans, and Celts, have sparked considerable debate in academic circles. Followers of Fell and Mahan believe it is only a matter of time before the history of America will be rewritten to take into account ancient cultural contacts with the Old World.

Said Fell, "The fact that ancient European writings occur in America ... presents a case that cannot be dismissed, and must now become the basis of a new evaluation of the course of American history."

Secrets of the Kensington Stone

IN THE LATE 1800s, as the 400th anniversary of Christopher Columbus's discovery of America approached, a number of theories were circulating about transoceanic voyages to the New World in pre-Columbian times.

Romans, Phoenicians, Egyptians, Welshmen, and Basque fishermen were only some of the people suspected of having sailed to America centuries before Columbus's epic-making journey.

But in 1898, while scientists and scholars debated the veracity of those earlier voyagers, a quiet Swedish immigrant named Olof Ohman unearthed a peculiar stone on his Minnesota farm that sent shock waves through the academic community.

Inscribed on the two-hundred-pound chunk of gray sandstone dug out from beneath a tree was a strange tale about a band of Scandinavian explorers—eight Swedes and twenty-two Norwegians—who had sailed across the Atlantic and continued westward across the New World to what is now Minnesota. According to the story, several explorers were killed in a bloody confrontation with Indians.

"We had camp by 2 rocky islets one day's journey north of this stone," the inscription read. "We were out fishing one day. When we came home, we found 10 men red with blood and dead ... [God] save us from evil ... Year 1362."

Written in runes—the alphabetic characters of Northern Europe during the Middle Ages—the inscription appeared to be genuine. Specialists were called in to study the huge block of stone, which measured almost three feet long, sixteen inches wide, and six inches thick.

From the very first, opinion was radically and irreconcilably divided. One side maintained that the stone was a crude forgery; the other side held that it was genuine. The controversy evoked a rash of stories about Viking landings and new evidence that Scandinavians had preceded Columbus to America by several centuries.

That the Vikings had reached the shores of North America during the eleventh century was considered a distinct possibility in the late nineteenth century. That such hearty bands of mariners could have journeyed inland as far as Minnesota, home to large numbers of modern Scandinavian immigrants, seemed remarkable, almost too good to be true.

And when experts looked at the so-called Kensington Stone, they declared it *was* too good to be true, that the stone was a crude modern forgery. Ohman, who denied knowledge of any fabrication or hoax, took the stone home where he used it as an anvil.

The story of the Kensington Stone would probably have ended right there had it not come to the attention of a Norwegian college student named Hjalmar Rued Holand. In 1907, Holand purchased the stone and spent the rest of his life defending its authenticity.

Despite his many critics, Holand did manage to have the Smithsonian Institution put the stone on exhibit in 1948 and 1949. One museum director called it "probably the most important archaeological object yet found in North America."

But other experts disagreed. More came forth to declare the artifact a fake, and it was soon hustled out of the museum. Among other arguments, critics noted that the stone's inscription was remarkably unweathered for its purported great age. Some also suggested that the wording on the stone was grammatically incorrect.

The uproar over the stone did little to dampen Holand's spirits, however. Until his death in 1963 at the age of ninety, he continued to champion the authenticity of the Kensington Stone.

Holand's death did not entirely end the controversy. Frederick J. Pohl, one of the more active supporters of the concept of Viking exploration in America, has continued to defend the stone's integrity in several books, as have several other scholars.

In a 1982 book, *The Kensington Rune-Stone Is Genuine,* Robert Hall, a professor emeritus of linguistics at Cornell University, asserts that the stone is real. Another defender, amateur Danish linguist Richard Neilson, has published a series of documented articles in scholarly journals, claiming that new linguistic evidence proves all the runes on the Kensington Stone are authentic fourteenth-century forms.

While the controversy continues, the stone lies in a modest museum in Alexandria, Minnesota, its secrets guarded by the local chamber of commerce.

Okefenokee's "Daughters of the Sun"

NO ONE REALLY KNOWS which European first laid eyes on the Okefenokee Swamp. Legend has it that Ponce de Leon discovered the swamp in 1513 while searching for the Fountain of Youth. Others say Lucas Vazquez Ayllon found it in 1526, while some argue that Panfilo de Narvaez tracked through the region in 1528.

A favorite theory of many researchers is that Hernando de Soto was the first conquistador to explore the vast swamp during his northern march through Georgia in search of a lost city of gold. Supporters of this theory believe it was here in the vast Okefenokee wilderness that de Soto clashed with Indians during the so-called "big battle."

It should be pointed out, however, that few scholars who have tried to reconstruct de Soto's route have brought it anywhere in the vicinity of the great swamp.

The first official record of Europe's entry into the Okefenokee was made in 1772 in a report issued to the king of England by surveyor William Gerard de Brahm. In the report, Brahm made mention of "the great Swamp Oekanphanoko," which he called "impassable."

In that same report, the surveyor referred to the legendary Fatchaskia, a mysterious race of people who lived deep within the swamp and were called "immortal" by the Creek Indians. Brahms went on to say that "this Race could neither be conquered by the Spaniards nor Indians, and that they have their Habitations in the middle of said Swamp, that they are sometimes seen without, but their Avenues are indiscoverable."

The same story was later verified by William Bartram in one of his travels through Georgia and Florida. According to Bartram's version, which he said he also heard from Indians he met along the way, the swamp was inhabited by a "peculiar race of Indians, whose women are incomparably beautiful.

"They also tell you that this ... paradise has been seen by some of their enterprising hunters, when in pursuit of game, who being lost in inextricable swamps and bogs, and on the point of perishing, were unexpectedly relieved by a company of beautiful women, whom they call daughters of the sun, who kindly gave them such provisions as they had with them, which were chiefly fruit, oranges, dates, etc., and some corn cakes, and then enjoined them to fly for safety to their own country; for that their husbands were fierce men, and cruel to strangers."

The "immortal race's" settlement was apparently situated high atop the banks of an island in the middle of a beautiful lake. But, said Bartram, the land was enchanted and invisible to outsiders.

All attempts to find the island home of the daughters of the sun "have hitherto proved abortive, never having been able again to find that enchanting spot, nor even any road or pathway to it; yet [other Indians] say that they frequently meet with certain signs of it being inhabited, as the building of canoes, footsteps of men, etc."

Bartram theorized that the occupants of this enchanted land could well have been the descendants of the "ancient Yamases," who fled the Creeks after a bloody battle at some remote time in the past.

Here, in the middle of the Okefenokee, the surviving Yamases could have "found an asylum, remote and secure from the fury of their proud conquerors."

Throughout the eighteenth and nineteenth centuries, travelers into the swamp enjoyed repeating the old legends, often embellishing them with imaginative flair. In 1819, one such traveler wrote, "The warlike Indians of the Creeks and Seminoles have a religious veneration for this immense desert; they say it is inhabited by aerial beings, who interdict the intrusion of man...."

The "aerial beings" supposedly inhabited some remote spot in the swamp unknown to other Indians. Said the traveler, "Their center is composed of high land, on which are erected their wigwams."

As for the other Indians, "not even one of their warriors would venture among the gloom of its shade, after sun-set, for the best American scalp."

Untimely Endings

The Demon Ax Murderer
of New Orleans

ON THE MORNING OF MAY 23, 1918, New Orleans grocer Jake Maggio was awakened by a loud moaning and thumping sound coming from a nearby apartment occupied by his brother and sister-in-law, Joseph and Catharine.

Thinking someone might be hurt or in trouble, Jake rushed over to investigate.

Nothing, not even the horrors of World War I raging in Europe at the time, could have prepared the young Italian American for the grim sight that awaited him inside that tiny apartment situated over the grocery store his brother operated. Sprawled across the floor in a pool of blood lay Joseph and Catharine, their heads cleaved open by an ax and their bodies hacked to pieces. Catharine's throat had been slit from ear to ear.

When police arrived they found the murder weapon—an ax, left inside a bathtub full of bloody water. The killer had apparently gained entrance to the apartment through the kitchen door, butchered the Maggios, then fled through the same door when he heard Jake coming.

The question everyone wanted to know was why—why would anyone want to kill Joseph and Catharine Maggio, two of the Italian-American community's best-loved citizens and friends to all?

The next day, banner headlines in the New Orleans newspaper proclaimed the shocking murders as the work of a "demon ax murderer." The name stuck. In the months to come, the demon ax murderer would strike again and again, leaving behind a trail of badly maimed victims and mutilated corpses.

Even though most of the attacks were perpetrated against Italian-American grocers, panic spread throughout the city. Terrified citizens started locking their doors at night and went to sleep with loaded guns by their beds.

According to some crime historians, the brutal slayings were the work of a serial killer, one of the century's earliest and most fearsome. Particularly troubling was the manner in which the killer cold-heartedly broke down doors or smashed through windows while victims cowered in their homes and stores.

Less than two weeks after the Maggios were slaughtered in their apartment, the bloodthirsty killer invaded the home of Louis Besumer and his live-in companion, Anna Lowe, both operators of a grocery store. Besumer survived the ordeal and for a while was suspected of having murdered Anna as well as the Maggios.

But when the murderer struck again two months later while Besumer was in jail, police realized they had the wrong suspect. This time the victim was a young pregnant woman, who miraculously survived several ax-inflicted head wounds and gave birth to a healthy baby.

On August 10 another grocer, Joseph Romano, fell victim to the mysterious attacker. His skull was split open, but he lived long enough to convince the police once and for all that Besumer was innocent.

Seven months later, on March 10, 1919, grocer Charles Cortimiglia, his wife Rose, and their infant daughter were brutally attacked by someone matching the demon ax murderer's description. The baby died, but both parents survived.

Several more suspects were brought in and questioned, only to be released when new attacks occurred while they were in custody.

Soon after the Cortimiglia attack, the *Times-Picayune* received a chilling letter signed by the ax man that warned of future attacks. The writer even gave the date on which he planned to attack—March 19, St. Joseph's Night.

Then the purported killer offered a strange promise—to spare anyone he came upon who happened to be listening to jazz music. He would prowl the streets, he said, searching out victims, and anyone found not listening to jazz would be punished with his ax.

Needless to say, the city of New Orleans was filled with blaring jazz tunes on the night of March 19—and there were no attacks.

Five months later, on August 10, the killer struck again, this time attacking grocer Steve Boca with an ax before fleeing through a broken-down door. On September 3, an intruder slashed Sarah Laumann with an ax while she lay sleeping in her bed. Six weeks later, grocer Mike Pepitone was found chopped to pieces inside his small grocery store.

The wave of ax attacks continued for another year or so, then ended as mysteriously as they had begun. Although no suspect was ever convicted, some investigators say the Mafia, which had targeted Italian grocers for protection money, was behind the whole gory business.

Chances are the truth will never be known.

The "Other" Mr. Lincoln

EVERYONE KNOWS THE STORY about how Abraham Lincoln "saw" his own death months before John Wilkes Booth's bullet ended his life at Ford's Theater on the night of April 14, 1865.

There is little doubt that the Great Emancipator possessed some kind of psychic power that enabled him not only to see into the future, but also to actually step outside his body and witness events from a distant time frame.

Over the years, dozens of books and hundreds of articles have been written about the uncanny powers of the troubled president. Predictably, the subject continues to intrigue scholars, scientists, and investigators of the paranormal.

What few Americans realize, however, is that the president's special gift apparently ran in the family.

Perhaps the most "psychically disturbed" member of the Lincoln family was his oldest son, Robert Todd Lincoln, who happened to be with his father the night of the assassination. Robert, who died in 1926, apparently never got over his father's untimely death.

For the rest of his life, Robert—who would go on to become a notable statesman, lawyer, and graduate of Harvard University—seemed to be haunted by a series of inexplicable psychic events that each time ended tragically.

In 1881, for example, the unfortunate son of America's first president to be killed in office happened to be accompanying another president, James A. Garfield, through a railroad station in Washington, D.C., when a crazed gunman named Charles Guiteau jumped out of the shadows and opened fire on the President. Garfield would later die from his wounds.

Two decades later, in 1901, Robert was invited to tour the famous Pan-American Exposition in Buffalo, New York, with President William McKinley, a friend of the Lincoln family. While Robert and the President chatted, Leon F. Czolgosg, an avowed anarchist, shot McKinley dead.

For the third time, Robert Todd Lincoln had witnessed the death of an American president. And for the third time he was made painfully aware of the special "curse" that hung over his family.

Never again would he agree to meet—or even be near—a president. Invitations continued to pour in, despite his reputation, but Robert refused to go.

Was the Lincoln family hounded by a curse as many believed? Did some kind of vicious fate stalk the famous president and members of his troubled family?

Even today there are those who say yes—that something strange and powerful indeed was at work in the White House during the Lincoln administration. Lincoln, who often reported vivid dreams of his own death and other disturbing psychic phenomena, apparently was both bothered and in-fluenced by that unknown power.

The most famous dream came as he rested on a sofa in his Springfield home shortly after his election in 1860. A few feet away was a mirror in which the president could clearly see his reflection.

As he nodded off, a strange sensation swept over him. He was suddenly seized with the notion that something was out of place.

He opened his eyes. When he saw his reflection in the mirror, he nearly cried out in fright.

"My face," the president later told a friend, "had two separate and distinct images, the tip of the nose of one being about three inches from the tip of the other. I was a little bothered, perhaps startled, and got up and looked in the glass."

The image vanished!

"On lying down again, I saw it a second time, plainer, if possible, than before; and then I noticed that one of the faces was a little paler, about five shades, than the other. I got up and the thing melted away...."

Although the president hadn't the slightest clue as to what had happened, Mary Todd Lincoln, his wife, did.

Mrs. Lincoln, who claimed to have the gift of prophecy, was deeply troubled by her husband's strange story. Even though she never saw the image in the mirror herself, she considered her husband's story significant.

Could it be that he had somehow "looked" into the future? If so, what did the double image mean?

A few days later she came up with the answers to those questions. Then she confronted her husband with the grim news.

It seemed, said Mrs. Lincoln, that the healthy, happy face the president had seen in the mirror was the "real" face, and that he would continue to serve out his first term in office. The second face, however—the one with the sad, blurred features—represented death.

"You will be renominated for a second term," the First Lady warned, "but you will not live to see its conclusion."

Lincoln was chilled to the bone by his wife's startling prediction. But as the years dragged by and the upcoming political campaign drew near, he forgot all about it.

The disturbing vision in the mirror was only one of many episodes involving Lincoln's alleged psychic powers. He would continue to dream, almost on a regular basis, often about his own death.

His most famous dream was recounted by Ward Hill Lamon, a close friend of the family. In the dream Lincoln became aware of a "deathlike stillness" about him, then heard what sounded like a large crowd of people sobbing inside his house.

When he rose to investigate, he found that the mourners were invisible.

"I went from room to room. No living person was in sight … I was puzzled and alarmed."

Determined to solve the mystery, the president entered the East Room. Before him "was a … corpse wrapped in funeral vestments." Around it were stationed soldiers who were acting as guards; and there was a throng of people, some gazing mournfully upon the corpse, whose face was covered, others weeping pitifully.

"Who is dead in the White House?" he asked.

"The president," someone replied. "He was killed by an assassin."

The "Mystery Graves" of Cedar Bluff Cemetery

THERE PROBABLY ISN'T a cemetery in America without at least one "mystery" grave tucked away in some forgotten corner, grown over with weeds and marked by a crumbling, nameless headstone.

For years, the people of Cedar Bluff, Alabama, have puzzled over their own mystery grave—or graves, since there are actually four such plots in the local cemetery. It is thought that the graves, once surrounded by a handsome iron fence, are related and contain the remains of two adults and two small children.

The fence is long gone, along with the original markers, but the question remains—exactly who are the people buried in the lonely back lot of Cedar Bluff Cemetery?

Over the years, many names and dates have been associated with the bodies. Then, about fifteen years ago, a local newspaper editor came across information she thought might explain the mystery.

While digging through a collection of old newspapers and early Alabama state papers, Mrs. Robert N. Mann, editor of the *Cherokee County Heritage*, uncovered a true-life horror story.

The deeper she dug through the historical record, the more convinced she became that the mysterious graves of Cedar Bluff were linked to a grisly mass murder committed more than 125 years ago.

Although the facts are still sketchy, enough details have surfaced to convince Mrs. Mann and other local historians that the four people buried in Cedar Bluff Cemetery were the victims of a crazed killer—an ax-wielding murderer who attacked a young family one night while they slept, chopped up their bodies, and then burned them for no apparent reason. The gruesome details of the crime were revealed on page two of the *Cherokee Advertiser* in a story dated October 19, 1866.

In those days the wooded hill country of Cherokee County was a wild, lonely place inhabited by only a few brave settlers and scattered bands of renegade Indians. A person could travel for miles among the gloomy forests and craggy gorges without ever laying eyes on another human being. So vast, so unexplored and desolate was this spectacularly beautiful domain on the edge of the Southern frontier that many an adventurer who entered it never came out alive.

Aside from the natural dangers—bears, wildcats and poisonous snakes—there were other risks as well. Armed highwaymen and runaway slaves roamed the countryside, preying on solitary travelers. Whoever journeyed into this remote wilderness nestled in the northeastern corner of the Alabama foothills just across the Georgia line did so at their own peril.

One day in the autumn of 1866, a young family set out to make a new life for themselves along the rugged frontier. Not much is known about that family today, except that their last name was Williams and they consisted of a father, a mother, and two young children, about two and four years of age.

They apparently came from Georgia and were headed for Guntersville on the Tennessee River to make a fresh start. At least that is what the newspaper reporter theorized from documents carried by the man named Williams.

Traveling by mule-drawn wagon, they got as far as Bogan's Ferry on the Chattooga River, about two miles from Cedar Bluff, where they decided to bed down for the night.

It is not difficult to imagine what wondrous and thrilling thoughts must have filled the heads of the young Williams family on that dark, cold night long ago. Huddled beneath their blankets, listening to the strange sounds of the forest and quietly dozing beneath a million blazing stars, they must have looked forward to the next day and their new beginning.

But sometime during that fateful night their dreams were cut short when an ominous shadow fell across their sleeping forms. In the pale moonlight the unknown killer struck, the blade of his blood-drenched ax flashing over and over again as it struck first one body, then another.

It wasn't until the next morning that a group of blacks found the mangled bodies still huddled beneath their shredded blankets. Everyone was dead—hacked to pieces— except the mother, who miraculously lived for a couple more hours. Unfortunately, she never regained consciousness and died without offering information about the killers.

According to the newspaper account, the group of blacks rushed to a nearby farmer's house and alerted him to the shocking deed. His name was Bogan—presumably, the man for whom the ferry crossing was named. Accompanied by neighbors, Bogan set off immediately to investigate.

When they arrived at the scene of the crime, some of the men in the party—all rugged frontiersmen and quite accustomed to brutal acts of bloodletting—were so shocked by the grisly sight that they vomited. Others wept and prayed for the souls of the slaughtered.

An investigation showed that each member of the family had been killed by repeated blows from an ax. It was obvious that the attacker—or attackers—had struck while the unsuspecting family slept side by side on the cold ground.

"After they were murdered, the perpetrator of the deed set the bed on fire, in which the murdered family lay, by which the man's feet and legs were burnt almost entirely off," the *Cherokee Advertiser* reported. "The children were badly burnt from head to foot."

Some papers found in the wagon indicated that their name was Williams, and that they were from Kingston,

Georgia. A Bible in their baggage revealed the couple had been married in 1861.

According to Thelma E. Slone, president of the Cedar Bluff Cemetery Association, a group of local citizens buried the mutilated victims in the local cemetery, then built the fence around their graves to commemorate their horrible passing.

No arrests were ever made. Ironically, the true identity of the killer—as well as the victims—remains another great Southern mystery.

The Tribe That Chose Death over Slavery

THROUGHOUT HISTORY, tales of mass suicide have captured the popular imagination.

When whole groups of people set out to systematically destroy themselves, the reaction among outside observers is usually one of shock and appalling bewilderment. Mourners and investigators are simply left shaking their heads, unable in most cases to comprehend the level of religious devotion, political conviction, or other dark inspiration behind such drastic and disturbingly final measures.

In the early stages of America's exploration and conquest, Europeans were often horrified when whole tribes of Indians starved themselves to death or took their collective lives in other ways rather than submit to their white overlords.

As confrontations between the cultures increased, so did the number of mass suicides.

One group of Indians, the Biloxi, threw themselves into the raging Pascagoula River and drowned when a vision appeared to them in the form of a mermaid commanding them to do so. The mermaid-goddess had apparently become incensed with her subjects because they had allowed outsiders into their midst—in this case two French Catholic priests.

Suicide, of course, was not the only thing killing off large numbers of American Indians. Diseases, military confrontations, and unspeakably brutal working conditions continued to take a grim toll on the lives of the dispossessed natives.

And as native American populations dwindled, it soon became clear that other sources of labor would be needed to work the gold and silver mines and tend the fields and plantations of the American South.

When the first boatloads of African slaves began arriving on the East Coast in the early seventeenth century, it became obvious that these hearty savages were much more tolerant of their condition in a white-dominated society than were their Indian predecessors. Whereas Indians refused to work and often ran away, black slaves went about their duties with surprising gusto.

Besides, should they decide to flee, where would they go? What would they do? The Indian knew the territory and could quickly blend in with any tribe he chose. But a black slave, unfamiliar with his strange new environment, would be unable to hide.

So, whether out of choice or resignation, black slaves rarely bucked the system.

One group, however, did. And they paid a grisly price.

They were the Ebo, a particularly spirited tribe of Africans who had been rounded up on the West African coast for the long voyage across the sea to the New World.

Even in Africa, the Ebo had developed a reputation for being a proud, fiercely independent people. When they suddenly found themselves in chains bound for slave plantations in America, a plan began to form in the mind of a tall, young chieftain.

According to a tale circulated among Seminole Indians, the Ebo had been en route to Charleston when they made a stopover at St. Simons, a sizable coastal island near the modern port city of Brunswick. While there, the shackled slaves quietly complained about the grim fate apparently awaiting them on the South Carolina plantations.

In slavery, they would no longer exist as human beings. Families would be split up, perhaps never to see one another again. They would become "nobodies" in their strange new homeland, leading an abnormal life and unable to go to heaven upon death because they had left the land of their ancestors.

A great sadness prevailed over the hundred or so Africans that night as they pondered their uncertain future aboard the cramped, disease-ridden vessel.

Finally, the tall chieftain stood up and announced his plan. Rather than submit to a life of bondage, he said, the Ebo tribesmen should take their own lives. They should commit mass suicide, go together as one to paradise. Paradise awaited them after all because it had not been their choice to leave their ancestral homeland.

The chief's radical proposition was not immediately well-received among the Africans. When the chief assured them, however, that happiness and freedom awaited them in "the world beyond time," the tribesmen decided death might be better than slavery after all—especially since they were going to be with their loved ones in paradise.

So beneath a pale, full moon they marched, the entire group, their chains clanking and clattering in the muted Southern night, while echoes of their soft chanting rang through the gloomy oak forest along Dunbar Creek.

One by one they shuffled into the swirling depths of the creek, and one by one their black, naked bodies vanished beneath the salty waves.

Nowadays condominiums and a waste treatment plant are located along the creek where the Africans are said to have drowned. But on still summer nights, when the moon is shining bright over Dunbar Creek, islanders claim they can still hear the rumble of low chanting and the grinding of metal chains echoing beneath the waters.

John Dillinger: Dead—or Alive?

ON THE EVENING OF JULY 22, 1934, a dapper young man wearing a straw hat and pin-striped suit stepped out of a movie house in downtown Chicago where he and two girlfriends had just seen *Manhattan Melodrama* starring Clark Gable.

No sooner had they reached the sidewalk than a tall, broad-shouldered man stepped out of the shadows with a gun. He identified himself as Melvin Purvis, special agent for the FBI, and ordered the trio to surrender.

The well-dressed moviegoer quickly reached inside his pocket, whipped out a Colt automatic, and bolted toward a nearby alley.

Several shots rang out. The fleeing man with the straw hat fell dead to the pavement, his left eye shredded by one of the rounds fired by three other agents working with Purvis.

So ended the short but violent life of John Herbert Dillinger, the most prolific bank robber in modern American history and Public Enemy No. 1 for more than a year.

Or did it?

Ever since that fateful gunfight outside the Biograph movie house, rumors have persisted that the man killed by FBI agents was not Dillinger at all, but a small-time hood from Wisconsin who had been set up by Dillinger's girlfriend to take the hit.

Eyewitness accounts and evidence revealed in the official autopsy lend support to the theory that the dead man was indeed a "plant." For example, pathological notes by Dr. J.J. Kearns, the Cook County coroner who conducted the examination, indicate that the man shot by the FBI agents had brown eyes. Dillinger's were blue. The corpse also possessed a rheumatic heart condition, chronic since childhood. According to his naval service records, Dillinger's heart was in perfect condition.

Furthermore, the man slain outside the Biograph was shorter and heavier than the notorious gangster and had none of the distinguishing birthmarks, wounds, or scars that Dillinger was known to have.

But there is even more conflicting evidence to suggest that the FBI might have shot the wrong man.

On the night of the shooting, a local man named Jimmy Lawrence disappeared. Lawrence, who had recently moved to Chicago from Wisconsin, was a small-time hood with a record who lived in the neighborhood and frequently went to the Biograph.

He also bore an uncanny resemblance to the man identified by police as John Dillinger.

In addition, a photograph taken from the handbag of Dillinger's girlfriend some time before his "killing" shows her with a man who bears an amazing resemblance to the supposed corpse of Jimmy Lawrence. Could it be that the girlfriend tipped the police off that she would be with Dillinger that night, then staged the date with Lawrence, knowing he would be killed and her lover would be off the hook?

Some investigators have suggested that is exactly what happened. Crime writer Jay Robert Nash, who has probably studied the case as much as anyone, theorizes that Polly Hamilton, Dillinger's girlfriend, and her roommate, Anna Sage, rigged the whole affair.

According to Nash, Ms. Sage, a forty-two-year-old prostitute from England, was in danger of being deported because of her illicit activities. To prevent that from happening, Nash said she went to the police and told them she knew John Dillinger personally.

In exchange for not being deported, Ms. Sage said she could arrange to have Dillinger at such-and-such a place where they could nab him—the Biograph theater, as it turned out. She even agreed to wear a bright red dress so she could be easily recognized.

While FBI agents watched and waited in the shadows, "Mr. Dillinger" and his two girlfriends sat inside the theater enjoying popcorn and soda along with the movies. When they emerged, Purvis and his fellow agents made their move.

Nash feels, however, that they shot Jimmy Lawrence instead of John Dillinger.

Nash theorizes that the FBI later learned of its mistake, but that J. Edgar Hoover was too embarrassed to admit it, in spite of the overwhelming evidence that his men had gunned down the wrong man.

What happened to the real John Dillinger?

Within months after the shootout in Chicago, Dillinger's gang was wiped out. Those who weren't killed in gunfights—such as Baby Face Nelson and Homer Van Meter—went to the electric chair.

John Dillinger himself, the man regarded by some Americans as a genuine folk hero because he robbed only from banks and occasionally gave to the poor, allegedly married and fled to Oregon, where he disappeared in the 1940s.

The Haunted Land of the Gullah

ALONG THE LEGEND-HAUNTED COAST of Georgia, there are places where islanders never go after dark, where certain words are never spoken, where people still practice rituals that seem as strange and old today as they did two centuries ago when the first boatload of Africans introduced them to the New World.

This is the land of the Gullah, an isolated region of brooding ghosts, shifting shadows, and quaint superstitions, stretching from the lonely marshlands of Savannah to the gloomy pine barrens of old St. Marys. Here, cut off from the mainstream of American life by ignorance and poverty, the customs and traditions of hundreds of ancient tribal kingdoms have been remarkably preserved to form one of the most unique cultures in the United States.

Known as the Gullah, the people who occupy these windswept islands—most of them descendants of slaves brought over in the early nineteenth century to work the great rice and tobacco plantations of the Southern tidewater—cling fiercely to the old ways. To outsiders, those ways may seem exotic and oddly fascinating; but to the Gullah, a deeply religious folk who worship a multitude of mystical gods, they are matters of supreme importance, not to be ignored.

For example, the handful of Gullahs who live near the fishing village of Darien in McIntosh County never sweep out trash after dark. To do so would be to sweep out the spirits of the dead—something no god-fearing Gullah would dare try to do.

At Harris Neck, a remote community that overlooks Blackbeard Island, homeowners put a broom across their front doors to keep out witches and wizards. The people of nearby Sapelo Island place knives and Bibles under their pillows to prevent blood-sucking demons from entering their bodies during the night.

No Gullah wants to hear the hoot of an owl or the plaintive cry of the whippoorwill after dark. To do so surely means a death in the community. Others turn pockets inside out or place shoes upside down to ward off evil. When he sneezes, a Gullah will wave his hand and shout "Far from you," an old Bakongo tribal chant designed to keep demons at bay.

Most frightening of all is an ancient Ebo belief that spirits will return to earth to haunt the living unless proper funeral ceremonies are observed. That usually means a proper mourning period during which relatives and friends of the deceased gather in a circle and rock back and forth while singing, chanting, and humming ritualistic refrains.

Wise mourners also anoint the corpse with three morsels of bread and three drops of water. Then, following an ancient custom still practiced in the West African nation of Dahomey, they place personal effects of the dead—pottery, statues, tobacco, clothing, photos, and even alarm clocks—on the grave.

Of all the strange legends of the Gullah, however, none rivals that of the so-called flying Africans. In her book, *The Lost Legacy of Georgia's Golden Isles,* Betsy Fancher attributes this tale to a half-formed myth born out of the oppression of slavery.

Quoting an old descendant of slavery from Wilmington Island, Fancher writes: "Lots of slaves wuz brought over from Africa could fly. Dere folks can fly even now."

Another Gullah, Burris Butler of Grimball's Point, adds, "Dey tell me dem people could do all kine uh curous things. They could make farm tools work for them jes by talking tuh em. And some of them could disappear at will. Wist! And dey'd be gone."

Old Shrimp Hall, who was born a slave of Jacob Waldberg on St. Catherines Island, said in an interview that his mother knew of a man and woman who could "work conjure and fly. Anytime dey want to dey would fly back to Africa and den come back again to de plantation."

The grandson of another slave, Prince Sneed of White Bluff, recalled other tales about flying men and women. He said that at one plantation, the overseer worked the slaves so hard that one day they "just rose up off the ground and flew back to Africa. Nobody ever seen them no more. My grandmother seen that with her own eyes."

Tales of witch doctors and the ability to "conjure" abound on the coast. As in olden days, conjuring—or sorcery—can be used for a variety of things, some good, but mostly evil.

Whenever a Gullah gets sick or injured, he goes to the root doctor. Modern researchers of conjure medicine are often baffled not only by some of the techniques used, but also by the recovery rate.

For example, Gullahs will tie their hair in braids or wear green leaves in their hair to cure a sore throat. Certain other leaves are said to ease the discomfort of broken ankles, while cobwebs, sugar, and sometimes dirt packed into an open wound will prevent infection. Salt plastered on a person's head will ease a fever or headache.

Isolated on the vast plantations, coastal blacks evolved a unique manner of speaking, a rhythmic, hauntingly poetic, almost incomprehensible dialect that is actually a combination of English and African. Many Gullah words, African in origin, have been adopted into everyday English usage.

For example, most Southerners call a tortoise a cooter. Near Timbuktu, it is called a *kuta*. Small wild horses that roam the coastal islands are known as *takis*, the West African name for horse. Gullahs speak of "toting" cotton, a word that derives from *tota*, an African word meaning "to pick up."

Sadly, times are changing in the land of the Gullah. As modern civilization continues to press in upon their habitat, many Gullah have been forced to adapt in order to survive. Today, there are Gullah doctors and lawyers, teachers and military officers. However, few remember the old ways; if they do, they often no longer practice them.

The Saga of D.B. Cooper

ONE DARK AND STORMY NIGHT in 1971, a frail, friendly young man dressed in a dark business suit and wearing prescription sunglasses boarded Northwest-Orient Airlines Flight 305 at Portland (Oregon) International Airport.

Minutes after takeoff, the man calmly handed the cabin attendant a note saying he had a dynamite bomb in his briefcase. The passenger, who chain-smoked Raleigh filter-tipped cigarettes and who appeared to be in his middle to late forties, demanded two hundred thousand dollars in used twenty-dollar bills.

"No funny stuff," he warned the stewardess, tapping his briefcase gently.

It was Thanksgiving Eve. Most of the thirty-six passengers on board the Boeing 727 were returning home for the holidays. As the plane bucked and rumbled through the storm, the last thing on anybody's mind was a hijacking.

The man with the bomb identified himself as Dan Cooper. At least this is the name that appeared on the passenger list. Investigators aren't sure who the skyjacker really was, where he came from, or what happened to him.

Only minutes after taking off from Seattle-Tacoma International Airport where the plane had stopped briefly to pick up the ransom money and release the passengers, Cooper bailed out from the aircraft and vanished.

Members of the crew were stunned. Only a lunatic would parachute into a freezing rainstorm at ten thousand feet in the middle of the night. Clad only in a business suit and loafers, surely the man died either on the way down or once he landed in the rugged wilds of southwestern Washington below.

"It was obviously not well thought out," commented Ralph Himmelsbach, a retired FBI agent who has spent nearly a decade investigating the crime. "It was stupid."

If Cooper didn't freeze to death on his way down, he probably died when he hit the ground wearing an "extremely fast" parachute provided by authorities in Seattle, said Himmelsbach.

"And he came down right smack dab in the middle of the woods in really rugged country," he added.

But there are those who insist that Cooper was not a lunatic, nor was he killed during the jump. In fact, say some of the air pirate's legions of fans, the entire escapade had been brilliantly planned to throw investigators off the trail. A few even argue that he took part in at least one other skyjacking three years later.

To be sure, Cooper's Thanksgiving crime was the most spectacular skyjacking in American history. It was also the only time that the skyjacker of a domestic aircraft has eluded capture.

Almost overnight Dan Cooper—or D.B. Cooper, as a reporter later called him in error—became a northwestern folk hero. Tales began circulating as they still do about the mysterious skyjacker, about how he survived the ordeal, assumed a new identity, got married, and today leads a quiet life somewhere on the East Coast.

Then, in 1980, an eight-year-old boy playing along the muddy banks of the Columbia River near Portland discovered a bundle of crumbling twenty-dollar bills. The serial numbers of the bills matched those given to Dan Cooper in Seattle nine years earlier; but those were the only bills of the air pirate's ten thousand twenties to show up.

Agent Himmelsbach speculated that Cooper either landed in the Columbia and drowned, or that he died in the mountains and the money was washed out.

Predictably, Cooper believers will have none of that. Each Thanksgiving, crowds gather at taverns in the Northwest to celebrate the anniversary of their hero's famous skyjacking. At one bar in Ariel, Washington, for example, some locals believe Cooper himself once made an appearance at a party in his honor.

One woman, identified only as Clara, claimed Cooper lived with her until his death from illness in 1982.

Perhaps the best clue to Cooper's fate came to light in 1974 when an escaped convict named Richard Floyd McCoy was gunned down in a shootout with FBI agents in Pennsylvania. A former Sunday school teacher and Green Beret helicopter pilot, McCoy had been serving a forty-five-year sentence for skyjacking a United Airlines jet for five hundred thousand dollars.

Investigators say that McCoy's technique had been virtually identical to Cooper's, down to the phrase "no funny stuff" in his note and parachuting out of an airplane. When captured, McCoy refused to confess to being the vanished Cooper.

Hell's Belle

WHEN ANDREW HELDGREN came across the ad in the newspaper's lonely hearts club section, his heart skipped a beat.

Wanted ... a gentleman equally well provided with a view to joining our fortunes....

For years the prosperous but lonely South Dakota farmer had been searching for such a companion to share his approaching twilight years. In 1907, sensitive, sweet women were hard to come by on the hardscrabble Dakota plains.

Soon after answering the ad, Andrew learned that the woman's name was Belle Gunness, a twice-widowed woman in her early forties. In graceful handwriting, the Norwegian-born woman explained that she owned a large, productive farm in La Port County, twenty-five miles from South Bend, Indiana, where she lived with her three adopted children.

Before long Andrew and his newly found love were corresponding on a regular basis. They couldn't wait to join one another.

"My heart beats in wild rapture for you, my Andrew," Belle confessed in one letter. In another she said, "I love you. Come prepared to stay forever."

In time the lovesick farmer sold his property, withdrew his savings, and set off to join the woman of his dreams.

But the dream turned out to be a nightmare.

Instead of the sweet, shy socialite he expected to spend the rest of his life with, Andrew found Belle Gunness to be a coarse, three-hundred-pound amazon who smoked, drank heavily, and refused to take baths. It was even rumored that she and her handyman lover, Ray Lamphere, had murdered her two previous husbands to collect insurance.

Through the grapevine Andrew also learned that Belle had secretly conspired with Lamphere to burn down the homes of her late husbands in insurance schemes.

When Andrew finally got up the nerve to question Belle about the rumors, she laughed them off, saying her first heavily-insured husband had died of a heart attack, and the second had succumbed after an accident with a meat cleaver.

Andrew had other questions, but before he had time to ask them he vanished—along with the three thousand dollars in cash he had brought with him.

Later, when Andrew's brother, Asle, inquired about his whereabouts, Belle's response was that the Dakotan had deserted her. She offered to let Asle come visit her farm and look around—if she were paid for her trouble.

Only days before his arrival, however, tragedy struck— Belle's house burned to the ground. Four bodies were found inside the charred remains—those of the three adopted children and what appeared to be the decapitated torso of Belle Gunness herself.

Ray Lamphere, the handyman, was arrested for murder and arson. Throughout the trial he swore he was innocent, that he was nowhere near the farm when the house caught fire.

Some people theorized that Belle had murdered her own children, set the house on fire, then faked her own death and fled the county.

When Asle Heldgren arrived, he made a grisly discovery. Buried beneath Belle's hogpen was the body of his brother, Andrew, along with at least forty others, most of them suitors who had answered Belle's ad in the newspaper.

Investigators then determined that the headless body found in the house was not Belle's, but that of a woman who had been killed so that Belle would be presumed dead and could flee with her accumulated riches.

Several months later Lamphere made a startling deathbed confession to the Reverand E.A. Schell. Over the years, he said, he had helped Belle bury dozens of men and boys, most of them victims of her newspaper ad scheme. Lamphere also confirmed what many already suspected— that he had helped Belle murder the children, then burn down the house in exchange for money.

According to Lamphere, Belle's various schemes and murders had netted more than 250 thousand dollars over the years.

She was never found.

The Strange Disappearance
of Tiffany Sessions

LATE ONE AFTERNOON in the winter of 1989, an attractive, twenty-year-old coed at the University of Florida in Gainesville slipped on her sneakers and sweatpants and left word that she was going for an hour-long power walk.

She never returned.

The strange disappearance of Tiffany Sessions, daughter of a wealthy Florida executive, touched off one of the most massive manhunts in American history. Not since Amelia Earhart vanished over the blue Pacific in 1937 had so many people and levels of government been involved in the hunt for a missing individual.

In the days and weeks after Tiffany vanished, hundreds of volunteers, many of them fellow students, combed rugged swamps and woodlands and probed rivers and creeks in search of evidence. They dug up neighborhood yards; they plowed up fields; they ransacked basements, abandoned tenements, and warehouses, determined not to give up their quest until either Tiffany returned or they found her body.

Since kidnapping was suspected, agents from the FBI soon joined the case. Four deputies from the Alachua County Sheriff's Department in Gainesville were assigned to the investigation, as were officers from the Florida State Patrol. Flyers were printed up by the thousands and distributed to the news media, stores, restaurants, and law enforcement agencies.

Patrick Sessions, Tiffany's father, bought television air time and space in newspapers to beg for information about his missing daughter. With tears in his eyes, the bearded father offered to pay any ransom for her safe return.

Even Florida governor Robert Martinez appeared at a press conference with Sessions, pleading for information to help find the missing woman.

To date, however, not one single clue has emerged to explain the fate of Tiffany Sessions. In the words of one investigator, "it's like she stepped off the face of the earth."

Not satisfied with the conventional efforts of the police and FBI, Sessions turned to famed psychic Noreen Renier of Orlando to help in the search. Renier agreed, but the reading she got while handling Tiffany's toothbrush was not a pleasant one—she feared a body would be found.

Meanwhile, investigators continued to respond to more than two thousand tips and leads. Not one of them led police any closer to solving the mystery that soon became the focus of several nationwide talk shows and scores of magazine and newspaper articles and books.

One Gainesville area man received a six-year prison sentence after offering to sell Sessions bogus information for two hundred thousand dollars.

Then, almost two years after the coed's baffling disappearance, a nightmarish horror descended on the quiet university community. While investigators still searched for Tiffany, the badly mutilated remains of several young coeds and at least one young man were found in their apartments.

One of the victims had been decapitated, her head placed on a shelf to greet visitors arriving at the gruesome death scene. Other body parts and ripped shreds of clothing were scattered about the blood-splattered apartments.

The wave of killings that shocked and terrified Gainesville and the nation would continue for several more months, as more women were reported missing and more mutilated bodies of coeds turned up.

Still there was no sign of Tiffany Sessions. Authorities soon began to suspect she might have been the first in the long wave of grisly killings that gripped Gainesville for two years.

Others weren't so sure.

Did she fall victim to the same crazed killer who descended upon Gainesville—or did something else happen?

Some investigators theorize she was the victim of a terrorist kidnapping whose plans went astray. Others say she might have run away with an unknown boyfriend.

To this day, no one really knows.

Jerrold Potter's Flight into the Unknown

JERROLD I. POTTER WAS the quintessential successful businessman—handsome, healthy, happily married with two grown daughters and memberships in several prestigious business and civic organizations, including the Lions, Elks, Moose, and the Kankakee, Illinois, chamber of commerce.

"He had it all," a friend and business associate would later remark, "a nice home, good health and lots of friends."

But on the morning of June 29, 1968, fate was poised to change all that as the middle-aged insurance executive climbed aboard a chartered DC-3 bound for Dallas, Texas, where he and his wife, Carrie, were to attend a national Lions Club convention.

It was a perfect summer day for flying—bright, sunny, not a cloud in the sky, pilot Miguel Raul Cabeza would recall. "There was no weather disturbance to account for what would happen later," Cabeza said.

Less than an hour into the flight, high over the rolling green hills of Missouri, Potter stood up, stretched, and told his wife he was going to the lavatory.

"Don't be long," Carrie Potter whispered to her husband, as she watched him lumber down the aisle toward the rear of the plane. "You don't want to miss the views."

She watched him pause briefly to talk with James Schaive, president of the Lions Club in Ottawa, Illinois, then turned back to the window to marvel at the stunning scenery eight thousand feet below.

Carrie Potter never saw her husband again.

Half an hour later when her husband had not returned from the lavatory, Carrie Potter began to worry. She glanced back toward the rear of the plane, saw the lavatory door still shut, then told herself to relax.

"He's okay," she thought, forcing herself to settle back and concentrate on the views outside the window.

A few minutes later the plane lurched, as if struck by an air pocket. It happened so fast that only a few passengers and crew members noticed the disturbance.

Then Cabeza saw the red warning light on the control panel. DOOR OPEN, the light flashed. A chill swept down the pilot's spine. "How about checking the emergency doors," he instructed co-pilot Roy Bacus.

It was about that same time that Carrie Potter had called out for a flight attendant to check on her husband. "Something's wrong," she whispered, so as not to disturb anyone else. "My husband must be sick or something in the lavatory. Would you mind checking, please?"

The stewardess went straight to the lavatory and knocked on the door. When no reply came on her third try, she opened the door and looked inside. The tiny room was empty.

At that moment she bumped into Bacus. "I think a passenger is missing," she whispered, then explained that Potter had last been seen near the lavatory when the DC-3 hit the air pocket. "No one has seen him."

A quick search of the plane turned up no trace of the missing passenger. A few minutes later Bacus walked to the back of the plane and got the shock of his life—the rear exit door was open!

It was only a crack, not enough to cause any problems aboard the plane, but unsettling nevertheless. Then he saw the safety chain lying on the floor. He scooped it up and headed forward.

Upon hearing the bizarre story, Cabeza theorized that Potter may have been thrown against the door when the aircraft lurched earlier, and, when the chain broke, fell out.

Cabeza brought the plane in for an emergency landing at the Springfield, Missouri, airport. A thorough inspection of the aircraft, including the door and stairs locked in the down position, revealed no clues to Potter's fate.

"He had simply disappeared," Bacus said.

What happened? How could a man be inside an airplane nearly two miles in the air and then not be there?

Did he commit suicide by opening the door and leaping out? Or, as some have speculated, did someone knock him out in the lavatory, then dump his body outside the plane?

Could Potter have mistaken the exit door for the lavatory door?

According to airline officials, air pressure would have made it extremely difficult for anyone to open the rear exit door in flight either accidentally or on purpose.

Despite a massive search on the ground beneath the DC-3's flight path, Potter's body was never found.

He was simply gone—vanished two miles above the earth.

Unusual Characters

Typhoid Mary, Angel of Death

THE SUMMER HOME of J. Coleman Drayton was a handsome, rambling estate nestled along the serene coast of Dark Harbour, Maine, where the successful New York attorney brought his family year after year to rest and unwind.

These were grand times for the Drayton family, who each season transformed their happy vacation "cottage" into a focal point for local social activities.

There was no reason to suspect the good times would ever end.

Then, in the summer of 1902, Drayton hired a new cook to assist in the kitchen. The new employee was a large, friendly, fortyish-looking woman who gave her name as Mary Mallon. Her twinkly eyes and warm ways quickly made her a favorite in the Drayton household.

Things went well for the first few weeks after Mallon's arrival. Then, in early July, one of the Drayton children complained of nausea and diarrhea. Two days later another child was confined to bed with the same bewildering symptoms.

By the middle of the following week every member of the Drayton household, seven in all, was suffering from the same unknown malady.

Only two residents escaped the illness—Drayton and the new cook, Mary Mallon.

As soon as the disease was diagnosed as the dreaded typhoid fever, Drayton understood why he had escaped the illness himself. A previous bout in the past had left him

174

immune to the painful disease that, in those days, ranked as the seventh leading cause of death in the United States.

What puzzled him and attending physicians, however, was: how had his new cook fared so well?

Since typhoid fever was a highly communicable disease passed on by infected individuals, investigators began looking for the original carrier. At first they thought it had been a footman, one of the first to come down with the disease.

It wasn't until several weeks later, long after Mallon had left her job and the state of Maine, that doctors linked the outbreak to Mallon herself.

Unknown to the Drayton family at the time, the friendly, hard-working cook they had brought into their home was none other than "Typhoid Mary," the notorious, almost legendary carrier who would go on to infect hundreds of Americans with the deadly disease before her apprehension and hospitalization in 1915.

Immune to the fever herself, Mallon apparently was unaware that she was spreading typhoid throughout New York City and parts of Maine and New Jersey. Fifty-three cases, some fatal, were directly attributed to her but authorities will probably never know the true number because of her steadfast refusal to discuss her past.

Typhoid was and remains a highly contagious disease, caused by the rod-shaped bacterium *Salmonella typhosa* which infects the lower digestive system. Most victims are infected by drinking contaminated water, but the typhoid bacilli can also be transmitted from eating food improperly handled by a carrier—as in the case of Mary Mallon. Everywhere she worked as a cook, beginning with the Drayton home in Maine, outbreaks of typhoid fever always followed.

On March 27, 1915, police finally apprehended Mallon and took her to Riverside Hospital on North Brother Island in New York City. Lawyers argued that their client was being held illegally, as she had committed no crime, and demanded her immediate release.

The New York Supreme Court ruled against the request, concluding that "while the court deeply sympathizes with this unfortunate woman, it must protect the community against a recurrence of spreading the disease."

On Christmas morning in 1932, a stroke left Mallon partially paralyzed. She lingered on for six more years as an invalid in Riverside Hospital, then, on November 11, 1938, quietly passed away at the age of seventy.

The Mad Hermits of Harlem

IT TOOK GUTS to go near the eerie old brownstone mansion at the corner of Fifth Avenue and 128th Street in downtown Harlem.

Not only did the place look haunted, but neighbors considered it unsafe and often complained about strange smells and even stranger sounds emanating from the ramshackle eyesore.

Local children called it the "Ghostly House"—apparently for good reason. With its shuttered windows, unkempt lawn, and bolted doors, the gloomy, badly dilapidated four-story structure no doubt stirred up visions of forbidden secrets and disturbing dreams.

Rumors flew about loathsome creatures stalking through the dark, drafty corridors. Many wondered what manner of psychopathic terrors lurked within the dwelling's dingy and crumbling walls—the diabolical creations, perhaps, of the famous doctor who once lived there.

But, as time would tell, reality was stranger than even the fantastic tales being circulated among the gossipmongers in the neighborhood.

Every few days a dark, stoop-shouldered figure clad in old-fashioned attire would emerge from the building and set off down the street dragging a large wooden box tied to a rope. The man, everyone knew, was Langley Collyer, a frail, shadowy fellow with wild, tousled hair who had once been an engineer and a classical concert pianist.

Langley lived in the house with his equally talented and mysterious brother, Homer.

But that was all anyone knew about the reclusive Collyer brothers, except that they were rich, talented, and grotesquely eccentric. For the past several decades, they had lived alone, huddled behind the drawn windows and locked doors of their grim domain.

Life inside the once-handsome mansion had not always been so bizarre. Years ago, before their parents died, the Collyer brothers had enjoyed an extravagant lifestyle. Their father, Dr. Herman L. Collyer, was an eminent gynecologist; their mother, Susie Gage Frost Collyer, was a well-born lady noted for her musical abilities.

The wealthy parents saw to it that their boys received the best schooling available. Langley became an engineer and an accomplished musician, while Homer received a law degree.

The family had built the house around the turn of the century in then-fashionable Harlem. In those days there were lavish parties, and music flowed often from one of several grand pianos owned by Mrs. Collyer.

But sometime between the old man's death and the early 1930s, an inexplicable shroud fell over the Collyer household. Horace and Langley, once proud and determined young men, began to withdraw, to retreat slowly from the outside world. Rumor was that Homer had suffered a nervous breakdown, and his older brother felt obliged to come back home and take care of him.

On March 21, 1947, an anonymous caller informed the local police that someone had apparently died inside the Collyer residence. Neither Homer nor Langley had been seen for weeks, the caller explained, and a strange odor was coming from inside their peculiar, silent mansion.

Responding to the tip, patrolman William Barker broke into the second-floor bedroom. The grisly sight that awaited him nearly took his breath away. Mountains of garbage and junk filled every room from floor to ceiling, as did stacks of old doors, slabs of marble, bits of discarded furniture, glass jars, bundles of newspapers and magazines and books.

In one corner of the room, buried beneath a pile of rubbish, lay the dead body of Homer, shrouded in an ancient Victorian bathrobe. Teams of investigators spent the next three weeks working their way through the ramshackle house, sifting through an estimated 136 tons of junk before they found brother Langley's badly decomposed body buried under a pile of garbage.

Apparently Langley had died some time before his brother, leaving blind and partially paralyzed Homer to fend for himself until he finally starved.

Among the more notable objects found in the house were seventeen grand pianos, several organs, a harpsichord, the chassis of an old Ford car, twenty-five thousand books, marble busts, priceless antique furniture, a canoe, and several jars of human medical specimens, including the mummified remains of a two-headed baby.

What unknown power compelled the once-handsome, talented brothers to completely close themselves off from the outside world, to spend the rest of their days as mad hermits surrounded by decades of death and decay?

The house is gone today, condemned years ago as a health and fire hazard. But the grim memory of 2078 Fifth Avenue lingers on.

The Buccaneer of Barataria Bay

DURING THE WAR OF 1812, an unlikely hero emerged to help Andrew Jackson rout the British at New Orleans.

With thousands of British troops fresh from the battlefields of Europe massing off the Louisiana coast for an invasion, Jean Lafitte—arguably the most notorious pirate in American history—put aside his marauding ways to help defend the beleaguered city.

For his bravery and patriotism, President James Madison pardoned the famed pirate for his past deeds.

But piracy ran deep in the buccaneer's blood. Unable to resist the lure of adventure and quick profits, the handsome, cocky, French-born pirate resumed his old ways. Operating from his new base at Galveston Island, Lafitte and his unsavory rabble of mutineers, deserters, and privateers quickly amassed a fortune estimated to be in the tens of millions of dollars.

Most of the ill-gotten loot came at the expense of Spanish ships sailing to and from Spain's Latin American possessions. However, a few American ships also were attacked, prompting William Claiborne, the governor of Louisiana, to offer a five-hundred-dollar reward for the pirate.

When Lafitte heard about the offer he laughed, then posted a five-thousand-dollar reward for the governor's own head!

Throughout it all, the Frenchman had maintained that his actions were perfectly legal, that he was only acting under authority of various Latin American governments to seize

Spanish ships. In fact, the Baratarians, as Lafitte's band of cutthroats were known, considered themselves privateers rather than pirates.

They claimed legitimacy because they held "licenses"— letters of marque—issued by tiny, newly-formed governments authorizing them to prey on Spanish shipping.

Smuggling and piracy were nothing new to American waters. Settlers of Roanoke Island, the first English settlement in the New World, frequently waylaid Spanish, French, and even other English ships while sailing across the Atlantic.

Such activities were praised and often rewarded by various heads of state, including Elizabeth I of England. Sir Francis Drake, perhaps the queen's favorite admirer, earned quite a reputation and fortune as a dashing, daring "sea dog."

In 1820, when the U.S. Navy finally caught up with Lafitte's fleet, the wily pirate managed to escape and sail away into legend.

It is said that when the blacksmith-turned-pirate abandoned Galveston, he took with him a personal fortune of ten million dollars. But legends persist that millions more were left behind, buried at various locations along the sandy beaches and lush lagoons of the Gulf Coast.

Nearly every city, lagoon, and inlet along the Gulf Coast today lays claim to Lafitte's treasure. From Galveston to Aransas Pass, near Corpus Christi, numerous discoveries of buried gold and silver have been reported over the years, each said to be part of Lafitte's fabulous trove.

Lafitte himself helped spawn the tales, boasting that at Galveston alone he had buried enough money to build a solid gold bridge across the Mississippi River. People living along the coast have been talking about the treasure for so long that it has become part of everyday conversation.

For example, if a man gains a little weight, he might be asked, "What have you got around your middle there— Lafitte's treasure?"

As for the legendary buccaneer himself, he supposedly died in bed of a tropical fever in 1826. Yet the story persists that he fell in a daredevil engagement with a British warship in the Gulf of Mexico.

A popular tale about Lafitte's treasure is that the ghost of the smuggler continues to wander the earth in search of someone who pledges to use the money for good rather than evil or selfish purposes.

Only then will the soul of the heroic "savior of New Orleans" finally find rest.

Stonewall Jackson: Hero or Traitor?

HE WAS A QUIET, gentle man who enjoyed gardening, studying the Bible, and taking long walks in the woods. Those who knew him called him dull. They often remarked about his strange obsession with peculiar diets, odd exercises, and quack cures for his own hypochondriacal ailments.

But when war broke out in the spring of 1861, the tall, bearded mathematics instructor from Virginia Military Institute would emerge as the South's most celebrated military hero—a "demon on horseback," as one biographer described the thirty-seven-year-old commanding general from Clarksburg, Virginia.

In battle after battle, from Bull Run to Chancellorsville, the man who prayed regularly and taught Bible stories to his slaves would dazzle the world with his brilliant, lightning-like cavalry strikes and punishing infantry assaults.

Of all the great heroes produced by the American Civil War—Northern or Southern—few compared with the wildly eccentric hypochondriac from Virginia known to history as Stonewall Jackson.

So many legends have sprung up about this dashing and daring Confederate general that it has become almost impossible to separate fact from fiction. Perhaps the most enduring story about him has to do with the way he acquired his unusual nickname.

According to some accounts, Jackson earned the nickname during the first battle of Bull Run in 1861, when a fellow

Confederate officer noted the famous general's courage under fire.

"There he stands like a stone wall," Brigadier General Barnard E. Bee is said to have remarked as he watched Jackson lead his men in one successful charge after another.

The Yankees were routed at Bull Run and the South had itself a major victory and a new hero.

Jackson's nickname soon became a household word. For the rest of the war, whenever rebel troops marched or galloped into battle, they often invoked the name of Stonewall Jackson to give them strength and courage.

Not bad for a dull, pedagogic professor known to his students as "Fool Tom" and "Old Jack."

Throughout his brief life, Thomas J. Jackson had been an eccentric and wildly contradictory man. A tender schoolteacher who doted on children, he would later become a pitiless disciplinarian who "would have a man shot at the drop of a hat," according to one of his soldiers.

Wherever Jackson went—into the countryside for rest and recreation or onto the battlefield—he always took along his prayer book and prayer table. Concerned about a mysterious stomach ailment, he kept his posture erect whether standing, sitting, in bed, or on horseback.

He was also mindful about his diet—a strict regimen of raspberries, milk, plain bread or cornbread, and an endless supply of lemons which he sucked, even in battle. (The source of Jackson's lemons is yet another mystery.)

On a bright spring morning in 1863, the mighty general fell. According to eyewitness reports, Jackson was killed by a stray bullet fired by one of his own men during the battle at Chancellorsville, Virginia—one of the first accounts of "friendly fire" in American history.

For the next seven decades, the South mourned her fallen hero. Jackson's name—as well as the proud cause—was kept alive with parades, festivals, and holidays. Schools were named in his honor, as were buildings, bridges, and babies.

Then, in 1935, a bombshell burst over the memory of the South's gallant son.

An army major named John Murphy stepped forward and claimed that Jackson had not been killed at Chancellorsville after all. The major swore under oath that the general had deserted during the battle.

The question on most people's minds was: how did the major know?

Simple, said Murphy, who claimed to have served with the general as a sergeant. They had both gone over to the Union side on May 2, 1863.

"We rode up the Plank Road to the Mountain, or Mineral Springs, Road, at Chancellorsville, and crossed the Union lines there," Murphy was quoted as saying. "Eventually we rode to Gettysburg, Pennsylvania, where we found a group of dead Federal soldiers. This was in July, 1863."

Murphy said he and Jackson put on a couple of dead soldiers' uniforms and assumed their identities before joining up with the 1st U.S. Sharpshooters at Gettysburg under the command of Colonel Hiram Berdan.

After the war, Murphy said Jackson went out West and became a scout for General George Armstrong Custer. A few years later, he added, the former Confederate hero served in the Black Hills under the name "California Joe" Milner.

In 1876 cattle rustlers shot and killed California Joe Milner. According to Murphy, it happened during an ambush near Fort Robinson, Nebraska.

"On November 1, as a lieutenant of the 14th U.S. Infantry, I buried this man, Jackson-Milner, in a lead-sheathed coffin at Fort Robinson military cemetery," Murphy swore.

Records on file at Fort McPherson National Cemetery at Maxwell, Nebraska, do contain information on Milner's death and subsequent burial in Section S, Number 5921. According to Burke Davis, author of *They Called Him Stonewall*, officials at Fort McPherson confirm the record of Milner's burial "but know nothing of the legend itself."

The Wicked Witch of Wall Street

ONE MUGGY MORNING in the mid-1870s, a shabbily dressed woman in her late forties strolled into a New York medical clinic and demanded to see a doctor. With her was her son, Ned, a scruffy, equally ill-clad boy who had injured his leg in a freak accident.

When the medical staff refused to treat the boy free of charge, his mother, a surly, beefy-faced woman, stormed out in a huff, dragging her injured son with her. A few days later, complications set in and the boy's leg was amputated.

Ned's mother never forgave the doctors and nurses at the clinic. It was their fault, she charged, that Ned, her only son, had lost his leg. It was their fault that he would have to spend the rest of his life hobbling around on crutches.

Fuming, she vowed to get even someday. That day came only a few months later when the clinic went out of business—forced out because of political and economic pressures brought on by Ned's angry mother.

What the medical staff didn't know when they declined to give free treatment to the boy was that his mother was none other than Hetty Green, the notorious "Wicked Witch of Wall Street," reputedly one of the richest women in the world and, according to legend, one of the meanest.

Hetty Green's reputation as a cheap, penny-pinching miser was legendary. Even though she had millions in the bank and owned at least eight thousand plots of land in New York City alone, she never paid a bill unless forced to. As an adult she never owned more than a couple of ragged old dresses which she had purchased at a second-hand shop, and never washed her undergarments, so they would last longer.

Although she enjoyed few pleasures in life, she relished going to the Chemical and National Bank of New York, squatting on the stone floor of the vault and counting her cash and dividends while munching on a raw onion.

As unpredictable as she was eccentric, those who knew her often trembled at her approach—for good reason. It seems that another of Hetty's favorite pastimes was destroying people, whenever and wherever it suited her fancy. Among her victims was her own husband, Edward H. Green, who had been the architect of her early rise to wealth. Green was ruined by his wife because he had once acted against her advice in buying railroad stocks.

Green was already a millionaire when he married Hetty shortly after the Civil War. When their son was born, Hetty swore to make him the richest man in the world. To achieve that end, she started putting aside every nickel and dime for Ned's future. She never willingly spent a cent, not even for bills.

Later, after her husband's death, Hetty flitted from one cheap boarding house to another to prevent the tax collectors and bill collectors from catching up.

Miserliness apparently was in Hetty's blood. As a child she had grown up listening to her wealthy parents talk only about money. Dinner conversations centered exclusively around financial matters, and her father was reputedly so tight that he once refused the offer of an expensive cigar for fear he might like it and lose his taste for cheap brands.

According to legend, the first sign of Hetty's own eccentric ways surfaced at her twenty-first birthday party, when she refused to light the candles on her cake because she didn't want to waste them. She was finally talked into lighting them, but quickly blew them out so she could take them back to the grocer for a refund!

Years later, Hetty would economize by writing checks on scraps of paper instead of using bank forms. She also went to bed before the sun went down to avoid having to burn candles—which she kept in her house only rarely.

In 1910, nearing the twilight of her life, Hetty Green turned all of her personal affairs over to Ned and grudgingly went to live with a friend, Countess Annie Leary.

For the first time in her adult life, Hetty lived in decent surroundings. Until the countess took her in, it had been decades since the so-called "richest woman in the world" had enjoyed a three-course meal or slept in a clean, comfortable bed with silk sheets.

But the thing that pleased Hetty most about the arrangement was the fact that she wasn't paying a cent for her plush accommodations!

Even in the countess's household, however, Hetty continued her miserly ways. Not only did she gripe about her friend's extravagant lifestyle, saying she would soon spend herself into the poorhouse, but she also clashed constantly with every member of the domestic staff.

When she took on the cook—a dour, ruddy-cheeked Dutch woman not accustomed to taking orders—Hetty Green had finally met her match. In a heated exchange of words, the cook had held her ground against the feisty old millionairess.

Soon after the confrontation with the cook, Hetty suffered a stroke. Over the next few months there followed several other strokes, each one nibbling away at Hetty's once formidable strength. An attending physician attributed the series of strokes to Hetty's clash with the cook.

On July 3, 1916, at the age of eighty-one, Hetty Green died, leaving behind an estate valued at more than a hundred million dollars in cash, stocks and bonds, and real estate. Despite long and costly efforts by the state to collect taxes on Hetty's fortune, the Wicked Witch of Wall Street had the last laugh.

Since she didn't own a home, it was impossible for the state of New York to establish residency. As a result, Hetty Green went to her grave with her immense fortune intact.

Selected Bibliography

Because this volume is designed for the general reader, I have judged it reasonable to give good but not comprehensive coverage of the materials upon which the data and their interpretation rest. Where possible, I have tried to make sure that both sides of each question are adequately represented in this section.

Perhaps the best place to begin one's study of the strange is with the works of Charles Fort—*The Book of the Damned, New Lands, Lo!,* and *Wild Talents*—all available in a variety of editions. Or you might wish to read *The Books of Charles Fort* published for the Fortean Society (Henry Holt, New York, 1941) available at most libraries. More about Fort himself can be found in Damon Knight's fine biography, *Charles Fort, Prophet of the Unexplained* (Doubleday, New York, 1970).

The best collector of anomalies of nature today is Daniel Cohen, author of *The Encyclopedia of the Strange, The Encyclopedia of Ghosts, The Encyclopedia of Monsters, Mysterious Places,* and *A Modern Look at Monsters,* all published by Dodd, Mead & Company in New York. Young readers might wish to check out the following works by Cohen: *A Close Look at Close Encounters, Dealing with the Devil, Ghostly Terrors, Supermonsters, America's Very Own Ghosts,* and *The Restless Dead,* all published by Dodd, Mead & Company in New York.

Erich von Daniken has written a series of intriguing books on ancient mysteries, starting with his international bestseller, *Chariots of the Gods* (G.P. Putnam's Sons, New York, 1970). Although he poses some interesting viewpoints, von Daniken's books should be read for their entertainment value only.

The late Ivan Sanderson is somewhat more reliable in his *Investigating the Unexplained* (Prentice Hall, Englewood Cliffs, New Jersey, 1972).

Beth Scott and Michael Norman have penned a fine collection of thoroughly investigated ghost stories in *Haunted Heartland* (Warner Books, New York, 1985). An interesting approach to investigating the paranormal is offered in Arthur Myers's *The Ghostly Gazetteer* (Contemporary Books, Chicago, 1990). This book presents a straightforward who-what-where-why-when-and-sometimes-how about hauntings in America.

Those interested in learning more about America in pre-Columbian times might wish to consult the following books: *America B.C.* (Demeter Press, New York, 1977) by Barry Fell; *Voyagers to the New World* (Morrow & Company, New York, 1979) by Nigel Davies; *The Secret* (self-published) by Joseph Mahan; *Fair Gods and Stone Faces* (St. Martin's Press, New York, 1963) by Constance Irwin; and *Digging Up America* (Hill & Wang, New York, 1961) by Frank Hibben.

The "wild side" of North American prehistory is examined in depth in a brilliant new volume called *Fantastic Archaeology*. The author is Stephen Williams, Peabody Professor of American Ethnology and Curator of North American Archaeology for the Peabody Museum at Harvard Museum.

Much has been written about the Vikings in North America. Two excellent introductions are to be found in Samuel Eliot Morison's *The European Discovery of America: The Northern Voyages* (Oxford University Press, New York, 1971) and *The European Discovery of America: The Southern Voyages* (Oxford University Press, New York, 1971).

Well before the Jamestown settlers first sighted the Chesapeake Bay or the *Mayflower* reached the coast of Massachusetts, the first English colony in America was established on Roanoke Island. In *Roanoke Island: the Beginning of English America*, David Stick tells the story of that fascinating period, from the first expedition sent out by Sir Walter Raleigh in 1584 to the mysterious disappearance of what has become known as the lost colony.

Legends of fire and flood, poltergeists, ESP, witchcraft, sea serpents, and other strange topics are chronicled in detail by Colin Wilson in two fine volumes: *The Book of Great Mysteries* (Dorset Press, New York, 1990) and *The Encyclopedia of Unsolved Mysteries* (Zachary Kwintner Books, Ltd., London, 1977).

Atlantis: The Antediluvian World, (Gramercy, New York, 1985) by Ignatius Donnelly, which is available in many editions, may be the most influential work of crank scholarship of modern times. Lewis Spence's book, *Atlantis in America* (Brentano's, New York, 1925) is less well known, as is *Lost Continents* (Dover Publications, New York, 1970) by L. Sprague de Camp, a more balanced discussion of the Atlantis theme in history, science, and literature.

An excellent book that examines ancient fossils in the New World and their impact on man's views of the past is *Mammoths, Mastodons, and Man* (McGraw-Hill, New York, 1970) by Robert Silverberg. Two similar books, now both classics, are *Strange Prehistoric Animals and Their Stories* (L.C. Page, Boston, 1948) by A. Hyatt Verrill and *The Strange Story of Our Earth* by the same author.

Burke Davis has assembled a shivery collection of weird stories for Civil War times in a book called *The Civil War: Strange and Fascinating Facts* (Fairfax Press, New York, 1982).

The ever-popular subject of reincarnation is discussed in scholarly detail by Hans Holzer in *Life Beyond Life*, a book that suggests that life does not end at death's door, but continues on in the form of reincarnation.

Finally, let me recommend another book by Daniel Cohen, *The Great Airship Mystery* (Dodd, Mead, New York, 1981), the definitive study of that topic.